TIME
The Year in Review
2009

Sunspot *The U.S. space shuttle* Atlantis *is silhouetted against the sun on May 12, 2009*

TIME

MANAGING EDITOR Richard Stengel
ART DIRECTOR Arthur Hochstein

The Year in Review 2009

EDITOR Kelly Knauer
DESIGNER Ellen Fanning
PICTURE EDITOR Patricia Cadley
RESEARCH Matthew P. Wagner
COPY EDITOR Bruce Christopher Carr

TIME INC. HOME ENTERTAINMENT
PUBLISHER Richard Fraiman
GENERAL MANAGER Steven Sandonato
EXECUTIVE DIRECTOR, MARKETING SERVICES Carol Pittard
DIRECTOR, RETAIL AND SPECIAL SALES Tom Mifsud
DIRECTOR, NEW PRODUCT DEVELOPMENT Peter Harper
ASSISTANT DIRECTOR, BOOKAZINE MARKETING Laura Adam
ASSISTANT PUBLISHING DIRECTOR, BRAND MARKETING Joy Butts
ASSOCIATE COUNSEL Helen Wan
BOOK PRODUCTION MANAGER Suzanne Janso
DESIGN AND PREPRESS MANAGER Anne-Michelle Gallero
ASSOCIATE BRAND MANAGER Michela Wilde
ASSISTANT PREPRESS MANAGER Alex Voznesenskiy

SPECIAL THANKS TO:
Christine Austin, Glenn Buonocore, Jim Childs, Susan Chodakiewicz, Rose Cirrincione,
Jacqueline Fitzgerald, Lauren Hall, Jennifer Jacobs, Brynn Joyce, Mona Li, Robert Marasco,
Amy Migliaccio, Brooke Reger, Dave Rozelle, Ilene Schreider, Adriana Tierno, Sydney Webber

ISBN 10: 1-60320-095-9
ISBN 13: 978-1-60320-095-0
ISSN: 1097-5721

We welcome your comments and suggestions about TIME Books. Please write to us at:
TIME Books, Attention: Book Editors, P.O. Box 11016, Des Moines, IA 50336-1016

To order any of our hardcover Collector's Edition books, please call us at 1-800-327-6388.
Hours: Monday through Friday, 7 a.m.—8 p.m., or Saturday, 7 a.m.— 6 p.m., Central Time.

To enjoy TIME's real-time coverage of the news, visit: **time.com**

Display on the bay *An electrical storm turns San Francisco's familiar Golden Gate Bridge and the
surrounding waters into a painting in light in the early-morning hours of Sept. 12, 2009*

Contents

1 **Notebook** Images
Visions from a year of sweeping change

18 Verbatim, 2009
Gaffes, laughs and the year's trendy terms

20 The Year of Living Boorishly
Oh, say, can you swear? Got it covered!

22 Reality Shows
Pop culture's Hall of Fame, 2009 edition

24 Commentary
Nancy Gibbs salutes the year's everyday heroes

28 **Nation** The Players
Who's who in the Obama Administration

30 Dr. Obama's Prescription for Recovery
A new President's ambitious agenda

34 Profile: Sonia Sotomayor
A Latina judge joins the nation's highest court

36 White House Backstage Pass
Life in the Executive Mansion gets a makeover

40 Profile: Michelle Obama
A First Lady masters an unexpected job

42 The Untidy States of America
Four states weather a year of crises

44 Profiles: Chesley Sullenberger III;
Richard Phillips
Two gritty pros display grace under pressure

46 The Last Brother
Farewell to Senator Ted Kennedy

52 Nation: In Brief

56 **World** Upheaval in Iran
Civilians protest an election they call fixed

62 Power of the People
An eyewitness account of Iran's turmoil

64 An Uphill Battle
The U.S. arrives at a crossroads in Afghanistan

68 Four Days in Baghdad
Can Iraqis unite to forge a common future?

70 Obama on the Road
An untested President reaches out to the world

72 China's Bridge to the Future
The Asian giant's game-changing stimulus package

76 A Plague of Piracy
The U.S. Navy and a gutsy captain earn cheers

78 Profiles: Mir-Hossein Mousavi;
Avigdor Lieberman
Two Middle East leaders face the future

80 World: In Brief

84 **Life** The World Fights a Flu
The H1N1 virus swiftly traverses the globe

86 A Long-Lost Relative
The remains of an ancient hominid rewrite prehistory

88 Profiles: The Venus of Hohle Fels;
Ida, Primitive Primate
Two discoveries enlarge our view of the distant past

90 Starstruck
The Hubble Space Telescope's cool new images

92 Science: In Brief

94 Rebooting the Motor City
Can ailing Detroit rise from the ashes?

98 Profiles: Evan Williams, Biz Stone and
Jack Dorsey; Bernard Madoff
A trio of Tweeters and a master deceiver

100 Society & Business: In Brief

102 Victory Laps
The year's most thrilling moments in sport

108 Sport: In Brief

112 **Arts** The Worlds Within
The spiritual journeys of two pioneering artists

114 Screen Gems
TIME's critics review the year at the multiplex

116 Urban Uplift
A nifty new park redefines lower Manhattan

118 Now Appearing
The year in the Beatles, Britney and Broadway

120 Profiles: Stephen Colbert; Susan Boyle
TV's political jester and a surprising new star

122 Arts: In Brief

126 Milestones
Recalling those who passed from the scene in 2009

136 Index

We, the people *A massive crowd fills the National Mall on Jan. 20 for the Inauguration of Barack Obama*

Images

□ A quiet revolution in the U.S., as Barack Obama takes the oath of office and becomes the nation's first African-American President. A noisy, surprising upheaval in Iran, as citizens protest in the streets in defiance of the nation's Supreme Leader. An earthquake shatters Italy, and a heroic airline pilot, exemplifying grace under pressure, saves 155 lives. These are the visions we'll remember from a year in which history's pace seemed to slip into a higher gear.

Hold on! *Two boys struggle against raging floodwaters in the streets of Manila as Tropical Storm Ketsana batters the Philippines in September*

Calm before the storm *Moments before taking the oath of office as the 44th President, Barack Obama gathers his thoughts inside the U.S. Capitol.*

Outside, some 1.8 million chilly spectators awaited his oath-taking—which was marred when Chief Justice John Roberts mixed up the wording

A daring ditch *When a US Airways A320 jet lost power in both engines after colliding with geese upon taking off from New York City's LaGuardia*

Airport on Jan. 15, Captain Chesley Sullenberger steered the craft into the Hudson River, saving all 155 passengers and crew

Twilight's green gleaming *Sergeant James Schwab of Apache Company, a detachment of U.S. soldiers operating in the Tangi Valley outside Kabul, tr*

ight-vision telescope on a highway nicknamed IED Alley, scouting for insurgents trying to plant improvised explosive devices

Outrage in Iran *The eyes of the world focused on the Islamic theocracy in June, as demonstrators protesting what they called a fixed national election*

staged massive street marches in defiance of authorities. Above, a black-clad police officer sprays a demonsrator in Tehran on June 13

Street cred? *Men in Baghdad watch new U.S. President Barack Obama deliver an address to the Muslim world from Cairo University on June 4.*

The President called for an end to "suspicion and discord" and sought a "new beginning" between the West and Islam

Aftermath *Laundry hangs on a line in the town of Onna hours after an earthquake struck central Italy's Abruzzo region at 3:32 a.m. on the morning*

of April 6. The quake, measured at 6.3 on the Richter scale and centered in nearby L'Aquila, killed 297 people and left thousands homeless

Some strings attached *Germans celebrated the 20th anniversary of the fall of the Berlin Wall and the reunification of their nation in October via a Fren*

eater troupe that guided two supersized marionettes through the city's streets. The pair, a girl and older man, united at the Brandenburg Gate

Last dance *Michael Jackson, 50, rehearses for his planned concert series in London, "This Is It," at the Staples Center in Los Angeles on the evening of*

June 23. Within 36 hours he would be dead. This is the last documented photograph of Jackson performing his electrifying dance moves

Verbatim, 2009

'To work out how to operate a television set, you practically have to make love to the thing.'

PRINCE PHILIP, the 88-year-old British royal, complaining about the difficulty of using modern remote controls

'Ma'am, trying to have a conversation with you would be like trying to argue with a dining-room table. I have no interest in doing it.'

BARNEY FRANK, Democratic Congressman, responding to a Massachusetts woman who asked at a town-hall meeting on health-care reform why Frank supports what she dubbed a "Nazi policy"

'I'd just been on a trip to Minnesota, where I can only kindly describe most of the people I saw as little houses.'

ANNA WINTOUR, editor of *Vogue*, on the prevalence of obesity in the U.S.

'Nobody wants to see a round woman.'

KARL LAGERFELD, clothing designer, after *Brigitte*, one of Germany's top-selling women's magazines, barred professional models from its pages in favor of "real women"

'Took 'em long enough.'

PAUL HOUSE, a 47-year-old former death-row inmate, on learning he had been exonerated after 22 years in a Tennessee prison

'I think the fatal flaw of a lot of people in politics is that they want to be loved.'

MARK SANFORD, South Carolina governor, who balked at accepting $700 million in federal stimulus money for his state. This statement was made before he confessed he was having a liaison with a woman in Argentina

'This was a whole lot more than a simple affair. This was a love story.'

SANFORD, revealing his relationship with the Argentine woman he called his "soul mate"; he then said he was "trying" to fall back in love with his wife

'I make up stories.'

KHALID SHEIKH MOHAMMED, mastermind of the Sept. 11 terrorist attacks, saying he lied when he claimed to know Osama bin Laden's whereabouts while being waterboarded during a CIA interrogation

'A perfect storm of ignorance and enthusiasm.'

A FORMER CIA OFFICIAL, characterizing the U.S. embrace of brutal interrogation methods like waterboarding in the Bush Administration

'We hate you guys, but there is nothing much we can do.'

LUO PING, a director-general at China's Banking Regulatory Commission, saying Beijing will continue to buy U.S. Treasury bonds despite concerns about the potential depreciation of the dollar

'When I look in the mirror, I don't see a female. I see a soldier.'

TERESA KING, who on Sept. 22 became the first woman to be named the top drill sergeant for the U.S. Army

'They should see it like a weekend of camping.'

SILVIO BERLUSCONI, Italy's Prime Minister, on the thousands of people left homeless by an April 6 earthquake

'I kind of like being a President.'

HILLARY CLINTON, U.S. Secretary of State, presiding over a Sept. 30 U.N. Security Council hearing on sexual violence against women

'I think I'd rather get run over by a train.'

MADONNA, on whether she plans to marry again. In 2009 the singer finalized her divorce from film director Guy Ritchie

'You give me a waterboard, Dick Cheney and one hour, and I'll have him confess to the Sharon Tate murders.'

JESSE VENTURA, former Minnesota governor, saying the former Vice President should be prosecuted for approving "torture"

'The only thing we haven't done is have sex.'

MATT LAUER, *Today* show host, on his friend Martha Stewart, at her induction into the Magazine Editors' Hall of Fame

'There is not a day that goes by that I do not feel remorse.'

WILLIAM CALLEY, former U.S. Army lieutenant, offering his first public apology for his role in the 1968 My Lai massacre. He spoke at a local Kiwanis Club meeting in Columbus, Ga.

Vendrification n.—The process by which New York City street food vendors are becoming more upscale

USAGE: "In a city accustomed to gentrification, perhaps this new phenomenon could be described as vendrification, with more expensive, higher-tech carts and trucks sweeping in and shaking up the culinary terrain."
BlackBook, Sept. 25, 2009

Narcotecture n.—The architectural style favored by Afghan drug lords

USAGE: "Stylistically, narcotecture is incoherent and dizzyingly busy. Residences are composed of clashing globe-spanning elements: Asian pagoda tiers, Greek temple columns, mirrored skyscraper glass, medieval-castle balustrades and parapets."
TrueSlant.com Aug. 20, 2009

Bumpaholics n.—Women who love being pregnant

USAGE: "Having babies isn't addictive in the way that alcohol and narcotics can be. But bumpaholics feel compelled to procreate for many of the same reasons that substance abusers turn to booze or drugs. Infants are dependent creatures. They can give their mothers a clear identity."
Women's Health, July-August 2009 issue

Funemployed n.—People who have found they enjoy being out of work

USAGE: "The funemployed write blogs, issue regular updates on Facebook and Twitter and devote entire websites to helpful advice on how to make the most of the U.S. government's $475 weekly dole check."
Times of London, June 14, 2009

The Year of Living Boorishly.
Americans act out and talk trash, from sea to whining sea

BARACK OBAMA CAME TO THE PRESIDENCY PROMISING CHANGE, BUT IT'S A GOOD bet that the former constitutional law professor didn't aim to find himself presiding over an unkinder, ungentler America. But so it was to be: as the year progressed, the fabric of civil discourse kept fraying, and by late summer, town-hall meetings on health care had become unruly forums for dissent. Obama noted, "There's something about August going into September that gets everyone in Washington all wee-weed up." But he could have been speaking of the entire nation. In September the ugly trend achieved lift-off as a cultural phenomenon, as a hip-hop star, a tennis champ and a South Carolina Congressman offered object lessons in oafish behavior.

And the Loser Is ...

... Hip-hop star Kanye West, the TIME cover subject once known for his unerring style but more recently famed for egocentric antics. At the MTV Video Music Awards on Sept. 13, West interrupted country star Taylor Swift's acceptance speech for Best Female Video to bark that the award rightfully belonged to singer Beyoncé for her hit video *Single Ladies (Put a Ring on It)*. Later in the program, Beyoncé graciously invited Swift, 19, to the stage to complete her acceptance speech. Note to Kanye: Put a lid on it.

Serena Eats Her Words

Serena Williams, 28, has always been more volatile than older sibling Venus, 29, but she stunned fans when she loudly berated a line judge over a foot-fault call at the climax of the women's singles final match at the U.S. Open on Sept. 12. Ranted Williams: "I'll f------ take this ball and shove it down your f------ throat!" Williams lost the match to Belgium's Kim Clijsters, and lost fans when she issued an apology the next day that seemed half-hearted. She finally got her mea culpa right the second time around.

A Civil Finale for an Uneasy Incident

Well, it ended nicely, with a so-called beer summit, but a July brouhaha over race traveled all the way from Harvard University to the White House. It began when Cambridge, Mass., police received a call that a suspicious person was breaking into a private home. They arrived to find noted African-American scholar Henry Louis Gates Jr., absent his keys, breaking into his own house. When a riled-up Gates, on left, accused Sergeant James Crowley, on right, of racism, he was briefly taken into custody. Asked to comment, President Obama, who often treads lightly in such matters, declared that the police had acted "stupidly." Oops! An abashed Obama invited all parties to join him at the White House to clear the air, and V.P. Joe Biden, far left, made it a foursome.

Two Words to Notoriety

It was the heckle heard round the world. As President Obama addressed a joint session of Congress on health-care reform on Sept. 9, Representative Joe Wilson broke the chamber's strict etiquette by yelling "You lie!" after the President (accurately) noted that his proposed health-care benefits would not extend to illegal immigrants. With those two words, the South Carolina Republican was transformed into a national political figure, loathed by Democrats and embraced by (many, not all) Republicans.

That Man in the White House

Mocking officeholders is a cherished American tradition, but the abuse heaped on the new President took strange forms. Barack Obama was derided as a socialist and a communist—no surprise—but he was also compared with Stalin, Hitler and Mao. When the President said he would give a nationwide video pep talk to schoolkids, a GOP state senator in Oklahoma accused him of trying to start a "cult of personality," saying, "This is something you'd expect to see in North Korea or in Saddam Hussein's Iraq."

Reality Shows. Another way we'll recall '09: in fads, feuds, follies— and those fabled 15 minutes of fame

Televised Confession Of the Year

Late-night TV mainstay David Letterman, 62, married longtime partner Regina Lasko, the mother of son Harry, 5, in March. Then, on Oct. 1, the comic stunned a studio audience by revealing that he had been the target of a $2 million extortion attempt by a man claiming to have proof that the CBS *Late Show* host had conducted sexual affairs with female staffers over the years. A contrite Letterman admitted to the affairs, without naming those involved, and said that he had quickly informed authorities about the blackmail attempt. CBS News producer Robert Halderman, 51, was arrested and indicted for attempted grand larceny. Letterman apologized to his staff and his wife, and his late-night slot at CBS seemed safe—for now.

Hoofer of the Year

It's delightful. It's delicious. It's ... DeLay? Since relinquishing his post as House majority leader in 2005, Texas Republican Tom DeLay has been keeping a low profile as a political consultant while he awaits his trial on the grounds of conspiring to violate campaign-finance reform laws. So jaws dropped when the House's erstwhile "Hammer" declared he would join the cast of ABC-TV's hit show *Dancing with the Stars*. Ignoring the jibes of his foes, DeLay gave it his all. "Headed to the studio for my first rehearsal and to meet my partner. Hoping it's not Nancy Pelosi :)," he tweeted. Alas, the viewers' gratification was, uh, delayed: the Twirlin' Texan withdrew from the show after only three weeks due to an injury.

Couple of the Year

They are such stuff as tabloid editors' dreams are made of. Jon and Kate Gosselin were already famed as the stars of TLC's hit reality series *Jon & Kate Plus 8*, which depicts their adventures in raising twins and sextuplets. But when the couple announced in June that they'd decided to separate, the TV show's ratings sagged—while tabloid tales drove newsstand sales.

CLOCKWISE FROM TOP LEFT: ADAM LARKEY—ABC; ABC; CBS—AP IMAGES; RICHARD DREW—AP IMAGES; ALARIC LAMBERT—AP IMAGES

Senior Citizen of the Year

Just when America's most despised demographic, the aging baby boomers, thought their lives couldn't get more dismal, another reminder of time's rigorous march arrived: Bruce Springsteen turned 60 and became an AARP cover boy. Other notables blowing out 60 candles in 2009:

MUSICIANS
Billy Joel, Lionel Richie, Ric Ocasek, Hank Williams Jr., Patti LuPone

ACTORS & ENTERTAINERS
Meryl Streep, Richard Gere, Jessica Lange, Richard Lewis

Belated Arrest Of the Year

On Sept. 26, fugitive filmmaker Roman Polanski, the director of *Chinatown*, *Rosemary's Baby* and *The Pianist*, touched down at the Zurich airport to find police waiting to arrest him in connection with charges of a 1977 sexual assault on a 13-year-old girl. Polanski, 76, was traveling to receive a lifetime achievement award at the Zurich Film Festival.

Mother of the Year

Her name is Nadya Denise Doud-Suleman Gutierrez. But everyone called her Octomom after she gave birth to eight children on Jan. 26, through in vitro fertilization. Originally celebrated, the 34-year-old later found herself scorned when it was revealed that the single mother had already given birth to six other children and was surviving on public assistance. But income from reality-TV producers eager to peddle her story is likely to pay her diaper bills.

Madonna of The Year

America has spoken: an anxious nation demands a Madonna 2.0. Sashaying into the breach was Lady GaGa, formerly the plain Stefani Joanne Germanotta, 23. Let's see: hit dance album? Check *(The Fame)*. Wacky, tacky, paparazzi-friendly outfits? Check. Gay icon? Double-check. We have a winner!

Judicial Replacement of the Year

No, we're not talking about Justices David Souter and Sonia Sotomayor. The judges who really count in the U.S. are the *American Idol* quartet of Scowlin' Simon Cowell, teddybear Randy Jackson, sincere newcomer Kara DioGuardi and designated softie Paula Abdul. So it was a major surprise when *Idol's* producers declared that Abdul would be leaving the show after a salary dispute and bringing in comedian and TV talk-show host Ellen DeGeneres.

Nancy Gibbs

Do-It-Yourself Heroes. In tough times, the virtues that truly inspire us are old-fashioned and unglamorous. Yet they're often hiding in plain sight

HUMAN BEINGS HAVE ALWAYS CREATED THE HEROES we need, from Hercules and Sherlock Holmes—whose supernatural gifts let them conquer mighty foes—to Underdog and the Ugly Duckling—whose transformations were themselves acts of heroism. Right now, when the headlines clang with catastrophe and confusion, it's natural that we'd be at it again, searching for heroes to suit the times.

First there was Captain Chesley (Sully) Sullenberger, walking the length of his sinking plane to be sure every last passenger was safely off. Then came Captain Richard Phillips, battling pirates in angry seas. And finally there's Susan Boyle, the unemployed church lady whose dying mother had told her to chase her ridiculous dreams of musical stardom.

Any one of them could be your Uncle Oliver or Aunt Florence, living lives innocent of fame until faced with a sudden test. Not much chance to prepare, other than a lifetime spent becoming themselves. Sully had 19,000 hours of flight time; he flew gliders as a hobby, had two master's degrees, studied crisis psychology to learn how to keep a crew on task in an emergency. "Me and my crew, we were just doing our job," he told the President, who had called to congratulate him.

Phillips, a former Boston cabdriver, didn't have any weapons to take on the pirates with, so he tried to trade himself for the pirate his crew had captured. But the pirates decided he was more valuable and held him hostage for five days, until the Navy SEAL snipers performed the Easter miracle that rescued him. "What they did was impossible," he said of the SEALs.

"They are superheroes." Which is what his crew said about him.

And then there is Boyle, the youngest of nine children, deprived of oxygen at birth, bullied in school, living what seemed an airless life with her cat, Pebbles. When she auditioned for a TV talent show in 1995—in the age of arrogance and affluence—she was scorned. So she sang karaoke at the pub and cared for her ailing mother until the day she died. "Mum was my life," Boyle said. "She was the one who said I should enter *Britain's Got Talent.* We used to watch it together. She thought I would win." Boyle arrived center stage, with her awkward dignity and eyebrows like live mice, and even then fame mocked her with the nickname the Hairy Angel.

Of course the song that made her famous is among the most miserable of show tunes, sung by a broken, destitute girl: "I had a dream my life would be/ So different from this hell I'm living/ So different now from what it seemed./ Now life has killed the dream I dreamed."

Except Boyle's dream was gloriously resurrected. Ashton and Demi, king and queen of the Twitterati,

This epoch rejects the glamor virtues: it calls for modesty, patience, perseverance, proficiency. We crave the company of ordinary heroes

tweeted about her, but she could not know this, since she has neither a cell phone nor a computer. All she knows is that there are now photographers camped outside her council house and she's been invited on Oprah and somehow she has made hard people quit sneering and cry.

Once a month the news gods have delivered these parables to us, gifts in a gold box reminding us where value lies. It's so much better to discover that Superman could be anyone; that everywhere you look, there are hidden reserves of majesty and honor and genius and luck. The stories wouldn't have worked if Susan Boyle had been a yuppie barrister or Phillips a SEAL himself. Their normality gives them wings.

The qualities these stories celebrate are telling. Competence—as manifested in a pilot with a perfect feel for his machine. Sacrifice—in a captain who would trade himself for the sake of his crew. Persis-

tence—in the singer who knew from adolescence that this was what she wanted and would allow no humiliation to deter her. These are, not by accident, the qualities Barack Obama, national life coach, regularly exalts. He commends the public for its patience, which convinces me that he has read the parenting books that instruct us to pre-emptively praise our children for the qualities we want them to develop. Any real recovery will require an "extraordinary sense of responsibility," he says, which just means we roll up our sleeves and clean up after ourselves.

This epoch rejects the glamour virtues: it calls for modesty, patience, perseverance, proficiency. We crave the company of ordinary heroes, especially now, when we're all on our own, thankful for small distractions from all the big threats we face. It's a karaoke moment: we can't afford a band, but we'll gladly sing of normal nobility all night long.

Nation

◻ A new President was sworn in, hoping to make good on his campaign promises of promoting change and fostering bipartisanship. But as his Administration struggled to address the aftershocks of the 2008 economic meltdown—with a pricey stimulus plan; federal support to keep U.S. automakers in business; and a campaign to initiate major health-care reform—the policies were strongly opposed by vocal, often belligerent protesters. Within months of a long-awaited fresh start, Americans seemed more divided and more partisan than ever.

Mad as hell *Distressed by growing federal spending, protesters gather at a "tea party"—tea for "taxed enough already"—in Charlotte, N.C.*

The Players

President Obama's key lieutenants include old friends, old foes and plenty of experienced White House hands

Rahm Emanuel
Chief of Staff

Age: *49 (all ages as of 1/20/09)*
Previously: *U.S. Representative, Fifth District, Illinois*
Party: *Democrat*

Summary: Washington insiders vie to top one another in describing Emanuel's aggressiveness and vulgarity. Barack Obama once joked that if Emanuel lost his middle finger, he'd be "practically mute."

Emanuel is one of three overachieving brothers from Chicago; older brother Ezekiel is an oncologist who serves as a Special Adviser on health policy to the White House; younger brother Ariel (Ari) is a noted Hollywood talent agent.

A veteran of the Clinton White House, Emanuel is often said to play the bad cop to Obama's good cop in pursuing the Administration's agenda.

Timothy Geithner
Secretary of the Treasury

Age: *47*
Previously: *President of the Federal Reserve Bank of New York*
Party: *Democrat*

Summary: The financial industry insider faced the toughest choices of any Treasury chief in decades. He got off to a rocky start but recovered nicely with an ambitious bank-rescue plan, proposals for far-reaching regulatory reform and deft handling of the auto-industry bailout. He also moved to shore up insurance companies. But the impetus for regulation has dwindled, the federal deficit is worrisome, and big banks are still handing out big bonuses.

Robert Gates
Secretary of Defense

Age: *65*
Previously: *Secretary of Defense, 2006-09*
Party: *Republican*

Summary: Obama asked George W. Bush's Defense chief to stay on, as Gates had won the respect of both Congress and the Pentagon. The former CIA chief cut funding for weapons he regards as outdated and pushed to ramp up the U.S. role in Afghanistan.

Eric Holder
Attorney General

Age: *57 (he turned 58 on Jan. 21)*
Previously: *Private practice; Deputy Attorney General, 1997-01*
Party: *Democrat*

Summary: The fiercely independent Holder argued that Bush Administration officials should be investigated for possible illegal actions during their war on terror. Obama was opposed, but Holder chose to proceed with his investigations.

Hillary Clinton
Secretary of State

Age: *61*
Previously: *Senator, New York State; First Lady, 1993-2001*
Party: *Democrat*

Summary: Obama's strongest foe for the Democratic presidential nomination in 2008 is thriving in her new position, though some are surprised that she appears content to take a backseat to Obama on the world stage. With him, she is restoring the role of diplomacy in U.S. foreign policy after the Pentagon led policy under Bush.

Valerie Jarrett
Senior Adviser

Age: *52*
Previously: *CEO, the Habitat Company*
Party: *Democrat*

Summary: The well-connected Chicago real estate executive is a longtime confidante of the President (and his wife) and appears to have his complete trust. Though her position is nominally described as involving "public engagement," she serves as a sounding board for the President on a wide range of domestic and political issues.

Jim Jones
National Security Adviser

Age: *65*
Previously: *Special Envoy for Middle East Security, 2007-09*
Party: *Undisclosed*

Summary: In choosing Jones, Obama took care to select a highly qualified veteran of Washington politics, who, like Robert Gates, enjoys the respect of politicians of both parties as well as Pentagon generals. Unlike some of his predecessors, the onetime Commandant of the U.S. Marine Corps keeps a low public profile, but insiders say he is deeply involved in forming policy.

David Axelrod
Senior Adviser

Age: *53*
Previously: *Founder, Axelrod & Associates*
Party: *Democrat*

Summary: The mastermind behind Obama's astonishingly fast rise from the Illinois General Assembly to the presidency is a former newspaper reporter turned Democratic political consultant. He was instrumental in forming the Obama campaign's Web-based, grass-roots outreach. Like Jarrett, he functions almost without portfolio in the West Wing, where he is regarded as a calming, politically astute voice.

Robert Gibbs
Press Secretary

Age: *37*
Previously: *Communications Director for Senator Obama*
Party: *Democrat*

Summary: Gibbs has served as Obama's mouthpiece since 2004, before which he was press secretary for John Kerry's presidential campaign. The Alabama native and North Carolina State University alum brings a Southern sensibility to a White House whose political compass points to Chicago.

Joe Biden
Vice President

Age: *66*
Previously: *Senator, Delaware*
Party: *Democrat*

Summary: The popular Biden served in the Senate for 36 years before agreeing to run as Obama's No.2. Though he has a tendency for verbal misfires, he brings a common-sense approach to such key issues as the U.S. role in Afghanistan. Obama charged the veteran of the Foreign Relations Committee with overseeing ties with pro-U.S. leaders in Iraq.

Dr. Obama's Prescription for Recovery. A new Administration tackles a highly ambitious agenda

NEW PRESIDENT BARACK OBAMA RODE A PROMISE OF change to his sweeping victory in the 2008 election. But when he took office in January 2009, he found himself a captive of the woes left behind by the previous Administration: most economists agreed that the economic meltdown that reached a boiling point in the fall of 2008 was the gravest such crisis since the great depression of the 1930s. Americans had watched with alarm as the Bush Adminstration bailed out some of the nation's largest financial institutions with the $700 billion Troubled Asset Relief Program (TARP). As Obama took office, banks weren't lending, housing prices were in freefall, the U.S. auto industry was dying, companies were laying off workers and the unemployment rate was surging.

When Obama's team declared that its first order of business would be to pass legislation creating an economic stimulus package whose price tag exceeded the TARP amount, Republican legislators and voters—who had kept conspicuously silent as the national deficit ballooned under a G.O.P. president—erupted in dismay. By April, worried Americans gathered at noisy "tea parties" to protest the deficit spending that was funding the stimulus package. The harsh economic realities hindered Obama's hopes of passing progressive social legislation and bred an ugly political climate, nipping in the bud the new President's frequently expressed hopes of creating a more bipartisan and civil tone in Washington.

Hard times *Top right, a tea party protest in New York City on July 1; above, the logo of the Administration's economic stimulus program. At right, "clunkers" exchanged by consumers fill a Detroit scrap yard*

JOB ONE
Stop the Economic Collapse

Immediately following Barack Obama's election, his economic team began working on the centerpiece of the new Administration's recovery plan, a huge economic stimulus package. In final form, the bill totaled $787 billion in funding, divided as follows: $288 billion in tax benefits and credits; $275 billion in federal contracts, grants and loans; and $224 billion to keep entitlement programs funded. Some $144 billion would go directly into state coffers for programs such as Medicaid, with $152 billion marked for infrastructure improvements.

Obama hoped some Republicans would support the plan, but GOP members of Congress blasted the bill as a pork-laden "Christmas tree" of Democratic pet projects that would send the national debt soaring. Yet thanks to their majorities in Congress, the Democrats passed the bill in the House, where it won not a single GOP vote, and in the Senate, where it won three. The President signed the bill on Feb. 17, in a major victory for his young Administration.

The President's team had promised to seek out "shovel-ready" projects that could quickly be funded, but it soon became clear that rolling out the funds would be a lengthy process. By the fall, some parts of the economy seemed to have stabilized: the Dow Jones industrial average and the housing market were showing signs of recovery. But on Oct. 2, the Bureau of Labor Statistics said that unemployment in September had risen to 9.8%, the highest rate since June 1983. The recession had proved to be even more intractable than expected, the White House said, rendering the stimulus package a safety net that kept the economy from completely collapsing rather than the job-creation program it was planned to be. And as President Obama observed, a recovery that did not bring back jobs was not a true recovery.

$787 BILLION
Size of the Obama Administration's economic stimulus package

JOB TWO
Save—and Retool—Detroit

One hundred years after Henry Ford unveiled the Model T in 1908, America's automotive industry, once the engine of U.S. growth, came close to melting down. Two of the nation's Big Three automakers, GM and Chrysler, were saved from doom in 2008-09 only by the intervention of the government: the Bush and Obama Administrations threw GM a $50 billion lifeline, and Chrysler received a $14.3 billion bailout. Ford Motor, the best-positioned of the three U.S. companies, took no federal aid.

Polls showed the American people were strongly opposed to the bailouts for carmakers, but President Obama argued that a massive failure of the U.S. auto industry would lead to the loss of so many ancillary jobs as to be unacceptable. Chrysler filed for bankruptcy and reorganized itself into a new entity in which Italian automaker Fiat owned a 20% stake. GM also filed for bankruptcy and shut down its Pontiac and Saturn divisions. At Washington's insistence, CEO Rick Wagoner left the company and was replaced by COO Fritz Henderson.

In the summer, the Administration's "cash-for-clunkers" program, which gave owners a federally backed cash rebate for replacing fuel-hogging old cars for more efficient new models, was a big success: more than 650,000 new cars were sold, keeping dealers alive and helping upgrade the nation's fleet.

$64 BILLION
Total federal funds sent to General Motors and Chrysler in 2008-09 to keep them afloat

Ouch! *A physician opposed to the Administration's health-care package needles the President at an Oct. 1 rally in Washington, D.C.*

JOB THREE
Reform Health Care

"This has been the most difficult test for me so far in public life, trying to describe in clear, simple terms how important it is that we reform this system," President Barack Obama told TIME's Karen Tumulty late in July, amid his Administration's full-court press to pass a bill overhauling the nation's health-care system. "The case is so clear to me. And when I sit with our policy advisers, when you start hearing the litany of facts, what you say to yourself is, This shouldn't be such a hard case to make, because the American consumer is really not getting a good deal."

Give the President high marks for effort: he had campaigned on a promise of change, and in his first year in office he aggressively pursued one of the key planks of his election platform, health-care reform. It had been 44 years since an American President, Lyndon Johnson, had succeeded in passing a new social policy, Medicare, that was as ambitious as Obama's anticipated reforms.

There was no doubt that America's health-care system was badly in need of change. For starters, the U.S. spends far more on health care than any other nation, an estimated $8,160 for each citizen in 2009. Canada, in contrast, spent $3,912 per citizen in 2008, and Japan

$2,690. Yet Americans are not healthier thanks to their expensive program: we live shorter lives and have a higher infant mortality rate than many other developed nations. And many Americans are completely uninsured. An estimated 46.3 million people, including 7.3 million children, were not covered at the end of 2008, and only a serious disease away from bankruptcy.

Few Americans disputed that the nation's current system was a mess. Yet the issue was so complex, the players involved were so deeply invested in the status quo, and the prescriptions for a cure were so politically divisive that the Obama Administration, which had

$8,160
Estimated amount that will be spent on health care for each American in the year 2009— more than any other nation

$2,690
Estimated amount spent on health care in 2008 for each person in Japan

Salesman *The President speaks out for his health-care reform proposals at an Aug. 20 forum in the nation's capital*

hoped to pass a reform measure by mid-summer, found itself in late October still fighting to hammer out a bill that Congress would approve before year's end.

Recalling the last Democratic President's failed attempt to pass health reform—the Clinton bill that went down in flames in 1994—Obama's team turned the preparation of the bill over to Congress, rather than handing over an Administration-written bill. The President laid out only a few broad goals to be achieved: universal or near universal coverage; lower insurance rates; an end to denial of coverage by insurance companies for pre-existing conditions. Given the uproar over his stimulus package, Obama also insisted that any reforms not add to the federal deficit over the next decade. The decision to let Congress shape the bill, if welcome on Capitol Hill, made for confusion, as a passel of separate bills made their way through both houses of Congress. And the President's refusal to lay down a set of highly specific reforms he would demand in a final bill, intended as a gesture of openness and as a way to allow the legislation to be shaped by Congress into a bill that could attract enough votes to pass, was perceived as indecisiveness by some Americans.

By mid-summer, the nation was in an uproar over the proposed reforms: opponents of the process seized upon a minor provision in some bills calling for voluntary end-of-life counseling for those interested and labeled it a government-approved form of mandatory "death squads" for the elderly. Many observers noted that at protest rallies against government "intervention" in health care, many attendees were senior citizens already receiving Medicare benefits. And, as had happened when President Franklin D. Roosevelt proposed the Social Security system in the 1930s, many conservative and libertarian voters opposed any further federal involvement in the nation's health care as an unwarranted intrusion into the private sector and thus a form of socialism.

When the White House launched a campaign of town-hall meetings on the subject over the congressional summer recess, it offered its opponents public forums that they gleefully hijacked, transforming them into raucous, rancorous arenas for vocal criticism

of the Administration. The air grew so ugly that the President decided to address a joint session of Congress on Sept. 9 to lay out the case for reform. Polls showed a favorable public response to his speech, but the bitterness of the debate was amplified when South Carolina Republican Congressman Joe Wilson shouted out "You lie!" as the President spoke, a signifier of the nasty national mood.

By October the furor had died down a bit, perhaps as a result of a brilliant strategy by the White House to allow opponents of the measure to shout themselves out, or perhaps as the result of sheer public exhaustion with the issue: take your pick. Three separate reform bills, widely differing in their prescriptions for an overhaul, had been passed in the House, and one had passed in the Senate. On Oct. 13, the Senate Finance Committee, chaired by Max Baucus of Montana, approved a version of yet another bill that the White House said was closest to its vision of a reform package. Senator Olympia Snowe of Maine, a Republican, voted for the measure, giving it an important stamp of bipartisanship. The bill did not contain the single most controversial item under review: the creation of a government-operated insurance plan, or "public option," that would offer an alternative to private programs, intended to drive down costs. Many Democrats insisted they would not vote for a bill that did not offer such an option. Nor did the bill mandate universal coverage, although it did propose to insure some 94% of all Americans.

As November approached and the Baucus bill moved toward a vote by the full Senate, there was hard bargaining on the horizon, the future of the Administration's most important domestic priority was far from resolved, and the President was still fighting the most difficult test of his political life—so far, that is.

In the arena *Sotomayor kept cool under intense Senate grilling, winning the praise—and vote—of influential GOP Senator Lindsey Graham*

Sonia Sotomayor

A second-generation American rises from a poor childhood
to become the first Latina to sit on the Supreme Court

WHEN JUSTICE DAVID SOUTER ANNOUNCED ON May 1 that he would step down from the U.S. Supreme Court, new President Barack Obama said he would seek to replace him with a Supreme Court nominee who had a "common touch." With U.S. Court of Appeals Judge Sonia Sotomayor, he got someone with a common touch and an uncommon story. Nobody expects you to make it to Princeton from a public housing project. Nobody expects you to be chosen someday for the Supreme Court when your father was a welder with a third-grade education. But on Aug. 6, the U.S. Senate approved Sotomayor's nomination, 68 to 31, with nine Republicans joining 59 Democrats in voting to seat her.

The confirmation came after Sotomayor spent four days in July testifying before the Senate Judiciary Committee, whose GOP members tried to portray her as a left-wing activist who would rely on her Hispanic heritage rather than the U.S. Constitution as her judicial lodestone. The Republican attack centered on Sotomayor's 2008 vote in a racially charged affirmative-action case involving firefighters in New Haven, Conn., and her remark in a 2001 speech that she hoped "a wise Latina woman, with the richness of her experiences, would more often than not reach a better conclusion" than a white male. Anticipating the heat, Sotomayor noted in her opening statement that the remark had been a rhetorical device that fell flat. "I want to state up front," she said, "I do not believe that any racial, ethnic, gender group has any advantage in sound judgment."

If the Republican attacks failed to gain traction, it's because Sotomayor's record shows she isn't a barn-burning leftist. She tends to write narrowly crafted rulings that focus on close application of the law. She resists rhetorical flourishes and sweeping philosophical statements. Altogether, she's a liberal jurist who will be replacing another mostly liberal vote on the court, that of Souter, which means her arrival there won't do much to change the ideological balance.

When he introduced Sotomayor as his nominee on May 26, Obama noted that he was not only impressed with her judicial record but was also drawn to her by her "extraordinary journey" in life. It could be said to have begun with a journey her parents made during World War II, when they moved from Puerto Rico to New York City, where their daughter was born in 1954. Sotomayor was 3 when the family found an apartment at the Bronxdale Houses, a city-owned development built to provide affordable housing to working-class families. Her father died when Sotomayor was just 9—one year after she was given a diagnosis of Type 1 diabetes, which still requires her to inject herself regularly with insulin. After that, her mother Celina raised Sotomayor and her younger brother Juan on a nurse's salary but still managed to send them to Catholic schools that prepared them for bigger things.

By 1972, the hard-working Sotomayor had moved on to Princeton, where she studied history. She once said that when she got there, she felt like a "visitor landing in an alien country." But she left with highest honors and a Phi Beta Kappa key. She went on to law school at Yale, where she was an editor of the *Yale Law Journal*.

After law school, Sotomayor worked for five years in the office of Manhattan district attorney Robert Morgenthau, where she prosecuted everything from petty drug crimes to felony assaults and murder. In 1984 she moved into private practice as an attorney with a firm specializing in business cases. When George H.W. Bush was looking for nominees to the federal district court in the Southern District of New York, it was a Democrat, New York Senator Daniel Moynihan, who recommended her. She was easily confirmed, but in 1997, when Bill Clinton decided to move her up to the Appeals Court, Republicans held off a confirmation vote for more than a year, fearing that she was on course to be a Supreme Court nominee. Their hunch was correct, but their timing was off. Twelve years later, Sotomayor became the third woman and first Hispanic American to sit on the nation's highest bench.

Sotomayor said she initially felt like "a visitor landing in an alien country" at Princeton

White House Backstage Pass

At once a family residence and a bustling office building, the White House moves to a new tempo as the Obama Administration settles in

Born to run *The President promised his daughters a new puppy when they moved to the White House. Enter Bo, a Portuguese water dog who was given to the First Family by Senator Edward Kennedy and wife Victoria in March*

Glide path *Used to rugged Chicago winters, Malia, 11, on sled, and Sasha, 8, at right, were ready for fun when snow blanketed the capital*

Diplomatic maneuvers *Advisor Valerie Jarrett laughs along as the President launches a charm offensive on a seemingly reluctant First Lady*

Preview *At left, White House pastry chef Bill Yosses shows the First Lady an array of fancy desserts to be served at the Governors' Dinner on Feb. 22*

Body language *Chief of staff Rahm Emanuel huddles with press secretary Robert Gibbs in the Oval Office, right, while their boss reads a memo*

Give-and-take
Trying to stay loose, White House trip director Marvin Nicholson plays catch with the President outside the Oval Office, at left. Obama's personal secretary, Katie Johnson, plays coach

Touchdown! *Obama is known to be more a fan of basketball than of football, but he played referee while watching the Super Bowl in the White House theater, right*

Michelle Obama

It was a long journey from Chicago's South Side to
the White House, but she quickly seemed at home

THE WHITE HOUSE BECAME AS MUCH MICHELLE Obama's stage as her husband's even before she colored the fountains green for St. Patrick's Day, or mixed the Truman china with the World's Fair glasses at a state dinner, or installed beehives on the South Lawn, or turned the East Room into a jazz lounge for a night or sacrificed her sock to the First Puppy. Of all the revelations of her initial days as First Lady, the most striking was that she made it seem natural. She did not spend decades dreaming of this destination, and maybe that's the secret. "I'm not supposed to be here," she says again and again. And ever since she arrived, she has been asking, "What are the things that we can do differently here, the things that have never been done, the people who've never seen or experienced this White House?"

Three generations (Michelle's mother, Marian Robinson, moved from Chicago to help out with the kids), including two adorable girls and a dog—no First Family has lived with the weight of hope and hype that has landed on the Obamas. Styles they wear fly off the shelves. Dog breeders from Germany to Australia couldn't keep up with the demand for Portuguese water dogs after Bo debuted.

Michelle is the first First Lady to make *Maxim's* hottest-women-in-the-world list. (She's No. 93; it probably wouldn't be proper for a First Lady to come in any higher.) Cameras with lenses that can count her pores from three states away are trained on her around the clock. When Oscar de la Renta questions her fashion sense—"You don't … go to Buckingham Palace in a sweater"—the response is, essentially, Well, what does he know? This is what a paradigm shift looks like.

Few First Ladies have embedded themselves so quickly in the world's imagination. And none have traveled so far, not just from Chicago's South Side to the East Wing but also from the caricatured Angry Black Woman of the early-2008 presidential campaign to her exalted status as a New American

Icon, as if her arrival would magically reverse eight years of anti-American spitballing, elevate the black middle class, promote family values, give voice to the voiceless and inspire us all to live healthier, more generous lives.

Not all those great expectations will be met. But some will. Put the First Lady in a room with black teenage girls and her message couldn't be more radical or more all-American: Anyone can be anything if they are willing to work hard enough at it. This is inspiration with an edge. For now, perhaps it's enough to recall that the great-great-granddaughter of slaves now occupies a house built by them, that one of the most professionally accomplished First Ladies ever cheerfully chooses to call herself Mom in Chief, and that the South Side girl whose motivation often came from defying people who tried to stop her now gets to write her own set of rules.

—*By Nancy Gibbs and Michael Scherer*

She did not spend decades dreaming of this destination, and maybe that's her secret to making it seem natural

Plain and fancy *The First Lady, 45 in 2009, is elegant in pearls but enjoys dressing down to tend her White House garden*

The Untidy States of America.
One governor strays. Another won't stay. California? In trouble. And New York? Seeing double

Alaska
A Rogue Governor Heads for a Larger Stage

The speech in which Alaska's governor announced she would resign her office 18 months before her first term in office was due to expire was a distillate of all things Sarah Palin. It packed the same gob-smacking wallop as her arrival on the GOP ticket in 2008, when the largely unknown Republican electrified the GOP National Convention in Minneapolis with a hard-hitting speech only hours after John McCain chose her to be his running mate. Sunlit against an Alaskan waterfront, the governor delivered a speech of departure as telegenic as her boffo speech of arrival. Rambling along in Palinesque fashion, she didn't quite tell us where she's headed, but she left no doubt that she remains in a hurry to get there. And then there was the strange timing of the event: Palin delivered her stunning surprise late on the Friday afternoon before the July 4 weekend, at a time when few Americans were following the news.

The reaction was predictable: scornful critics called Palin a quitter; worshipful admirers hailed her decision as the first step toward her election as President in 2012. Either way, Palin's first stop was clear: she was going to the bank. She had already announced plans to write a book and had received an advance reportedly in the millions. (*Going Rogue: An American Life,* was finished ahead of schedule and published in November). A celebrity of her wattage commands big money on the lecture circuit; she received a reported six-figure fee for her first major address on Sept. 23 to investors in Hong Kong, which was closed to the media. And television may beckon: attractive and garrulous, Palin seems born to host a cable-TV show. While she blamed the usual suspects for her abrupt exit—expensive "distractions" foisted upon her by a biased mass media and aggressive Democrats—Palin's resignation will give her time to devote herself to the national stage. In contrast, concentrating on agriculture in the Yukon may have seemed mighty small potatoes.

South Carolina
A Governor Who Won't Take a Hike

When South Carolina's Governor Mark Sanford strays, he thinks so big he needs a GPS. In June, he told his staff he would be hiking the Appalachian Trail over the Father's Day weekend, a curious decision for a married father of four boys. Instead, Sanford hopped a jet and landed in Buenos Aires, where he canoodled with an Argentine woman he had met in 2001. But a reporter met him at the airport when he returned, and the jig was up. On June 24, the Republican who had harbored hopes for the presidency gave a rambling, tearful press conference, left, that won him few sympathizers. Perhaps it was his comment, "I don't know how this whole thing got blown out of proportion," that irked his constituents. Wife Jenny soon said the two would begin a trial separation. Republicans in the state assembly called for a more permanent separation, but as of late October, Sanford was yet to resign himself to resignation.

California
The Golden State: Saved—but Shriveled

Governor Arnold Schwarzenegger knows the political risks of budget crises: he rode to victory in a recall election when predecessor Gray Davis was hamstrung by a budget crunch in 2003. But faced with a $26.3 billion budget shortfall, Arnold and California legislators couldn't find common ground and, on July 2, the state began issuing IOUs to its creditors. Finally, on July 20, a deal was struck to close the deficit with deep cuts that will profoundly reduce the state government's size and a broad array of its programs. Hardest hit: local governments, the higher-education system, the public schools, tens of thousands of seniors and children who will lose access to health care, and most state workers, whose hours will be reduced. Republican legislators boasted of thwarting tax hikes, while Democrats said the state's safety net for its poorest was still in place.

New York
Double-Crosses and Double Sessions

Straying governors? Been there. Last-minute deals to avert bankruptcy? Done that. So New York State legislators act out more creatively. In the closely divided state senate, two rogue Democrats, Hiram Monserrate, left, and Pedro Espada, right, joined the Republican caucus, handing control of the Senate to the GOP, 32 to 30. Republicans rejoiced—until a few days later, when Monserrate returned to the Dems, evenly dividing the chamber. The state had no Lieutenant Governor to break Senate ties, as David Paterson had vacated the post, becoming governor after the errant Eliot Spitzer resigned in 2008. The madness peaked on June 23, when the two party caucuses held simultaneous sessions in the Senate chamber, each insisting it was the lawful state body. Solution: Espada flipped back to the Democrats—and was awarded the post of majority leader for his pains. Nice!

Chesley B. Sullenberger

A veteran airline pilot helped write the book on airline safety.
And then, displaying supreme grace under pressure, he lived it

AFTER LOGGING SOME 19,000 HOURS OF ACCLAIMED but anonymous service in the skies, Chesley B. Sullenberger III became a hero in a New York minute. On Jan. 15, 2009, the pilot, known as "Sully," safely guided US Airways Flight 1549 to an emergency water landing in the city's frigid Hudson River. The Airbus A320's twin engines had shut down soon after sucking in a flock of birds shortly after take-off from New York City's LaGuardia Airport en route to Charlotte, N.C. With both engines out, Sullenberger found himself fighting to keep the big jet aloft while gliding over one of the most densely peopled cities in the world, with only moments to concoct and execute a powerless emergency landing.

"It was the worst, sickening, pit-of-your-stomach, falling-through-the-floor feeling I've ever felt in my life," the veteran captain later recalled. He briefly discussed trying to land at a nearby New Jersey airport with a flight traffic controller, but time—and gravity—forbade that. Sullenberger quickly decided that his best course of action was to ditch the plane in the Hudson River. "Brace for impact," he instructed the passengers and cabin crew. Said Adam Weiner, an MTV employee who saw the incident from his midtown Manhattan office building: "I was sitting in a conference room on the 39th floor, facing the window. All of a sudden I see a plane gliding into a river. At first I didn't realize what I was seeing. Then spray went up, and you could tell it was a jetliner. Then a couple seconds after, the door blew off and you could see the raft blow up."

In the suspenseful moments that followed, passengers and crew clambered into the raft and onto the wing of the plane, and quick-thinking personnel of boats plying New York Harbor formed an emergency armada of rescue vessels to take them to safety. Meanwhile, within the craft, the steady Sullenberger walked the length of the plane as it slowly sank into the water—not once but twice—ensuring that each of the 155 passengers and crew aboard had exited the craft. He was the last person to be plucked from the plane, which was then towed to safety. New York Governor David Paterson described the safe ditching as the "miracle on the Hudson," and Americans agreed.

Sullenberger, 57 at the time, seemed to have spent his life preparing for this test. A 1973 graduate of the Air Force Academy, he served nearly seven years as an Air Force fighter pilot, attaining the rank of captain. He had been a flight instructor and the Air Line Pilots Association safety chairman, had investigated aviation accidents for the Air Force and the National Transportation Safety Board, and had helped develop protocols for airline safety. "I just can't believe how well he did. We're all alive because of him," passenger Beth McHugh, 64, told MSNBC.com. That was no exaggeration—nor is it an exaggeration to hail Sullenberger as an authentic hero.

Steady hand *Sullenberger's decision to ditch his jet in the Hudson saved 155 lives*

Safe at home
Phillips reunites with his son Daniel and daughter Mariah in Vermont

PROFILE

Captain Richard Phillips

With his ship captured by pirates off the coast of Somalia,
he traded his life for that of his crew—and survived

LIKE MOST AMERICANS, I CLOSELY FOLLOWED THE gripping story of the *Maersk Alabama*. The saga of the brave crew fighting off pirates armed with assault rifles read like an espionage thriller, but it was all too real. It was a sobering, cautionary tale for sailors all over the world, and an awful ordeal for the crew's families as they awaited news.

I was deeply moved by the remarkable selflessness exhibited by Captain Richard Phillips, 53. To protect his crew, Captain Phillips made a conscious decision to put himself directly in harm's way, knowing full well that he might pay the ultimate price for his decision. Held hostage as a human shield in a small lifeboat with three pirates, he had little to hope for or cling to—except the knowledge that he had done absolutely everything he could to save the lives of the 20 sailors aboard his ship.

My family and I have had the opportunity to think quite a bit about the word hero this year. My wife Lorrie said it best: A hero is a person who makes a conscious decision to run into a burning building, a person who places the safety of others above their own. While sailing in lawless, treacherous waters off the coast of Somalia, Captain Phillips offered himself up as a defenseless hostage in order to free his crew. He is a leader, a human being and, yes, a hero of the highest order. I salute him.

—*Chesley B. Sullenberger*

The Last Brother

Shouldering a burden of family expectations, Ted Kennedy struggled to greatness—and helped change America

THERE WAS A TIME 40 YEARS AGO, RIGHT after the assassination of his older brother Robert, when it looked as if Edward M. (Ted) Kennedy would become President someday by right of succession. The Kennedy curse, the one that had seen all three of his brothers cut down in their prime, had created for him a sort of Kennedy prerogative, or at least the illusion of one, an inevitable claim on the White House. For years he seemed like a man simply waiting for the right moment to take what everybody knew was coming his way.

Everybody was wrong. Ted Kennedy would never reach the White House. His weaknesses—and the long shadow of Chappaquiddick—were an obstacle that even his strengths couldn't overcome. But his failure to get to the presidency opened the way to the true fulfillment of his gifts, which was to become one of the greatest legislators in American history. By the time of his death on Aug. 25 in Hyannis Port at the age of 77, he had 46 working years in Congress, time enough to leave his imprint on everything from the Voting Rights Act of 1965 to the

Edward M. Kennedy Serve America Act of 2009, a law that expands support for national community-service programs. Over the years, Kennedy was a force behind the Freedom of Information Act, the Occupational Safety and Health Act, and the Americans with Disabilities Act. He helped Soviet dissidents and fought apartheid. Above all, he conducted a four-decade crusade for universal health coverage, a poignant one toward the end as the country watched him struggle with a brain tumor. But along the way, he vastly expanded the network of neighborhood clinics, virtually invented the COBRA system for portable insurance and helped create the laws that provide Medicare prescriptions and family leave.

And for most of that time, he went forward against great odds, the voice of progressivism in a conservative age. In the last year of his life, with the Inauguration of Barack Obama, he had the satisfaction of seeing a big part of that dream fulfilled. Early in 2008, he had enthusiastically endorsed the young Senator from Illinois, helping propel Obama to the Democratic nomination and ultimately the White House.

Favorite son *Senator Ted Kennedy addresses cheering delegates at the Democratic National Convention in Boston in 2004*

His marriage to Victoria Reggie transformed Kennedy, making him more stable and content

Band of brothers

From his father Joseph P. Kennedy, Ted inherited a burden of dreams. The Boston business magnate envisioned a dynasty, crowned when one of his four boys would be President of the U.S. This was the atmosphere that Ted was born into on Feb. 22, 1932—the last of the nine Kennedy children. Overweight and lonely, Ted was shuttled through a succession of boarding and day schools, but he grew into an athletic, good-looking teenager, one who ambled into Harvard, where brothers John F. (Jack) and Bobby had gone before him. But as a freshman, Ted asked a friend to take a Spanish exam for him. The surrogate was caught, and both boys were expelled.

After two years of military service, Ted returned to Harvard, majoring in government. He studied law at the University of Virginia, where he met and quickly married Joan Bennett. He began learning the family business, politics, by working on brother Jack's 1958 bid for a second term as Senator. After Jack became President, Ted won his Senate seat in 1962. He had been there for less than a year when J.F.K. was assassinated.

Jack's death was more than a personal tragedy for Ted. It was a watershed that put him one step closer to assuming the Kennedy burden, the quest for the heights. He helped pass the civil rights bill J.F.K. had introduced before his death, and then, despite a plane crash that sidelined him for months, he helped pass bills reforming immigration and beginning federal support for neighborhood clinics, his first encounter with the issue that became his signature crusade, health care.

By 1967, Kennedy had also begun to speak out against the Vietnam War—the cause that led his brother Robert to seek the presidency in 1968. Then Bobby was shot down as well. His death was a crucial moment of recognition for Ted that the burden of the Kennedy legacy was now his to shoulder. At 36, he was the last of the line. There was no one else.

Thirteen months after Bobby's death, on July 18, 1969, Kennedy hosted a reunion for six women who had worked on Bobby's presidential campaign on Chappaquiddick Island, just off Martha's Vineyard. Ted left the party with Mary Jo Kopechne, 28, a former aide to his brother. According to his later testimony, he took a wrong turn onto an unlit dirt road and then across a small wooden bridge without rails. His car went over the side of the bridge and landed upside down in the water. Kennedy managed to escape. Kopechne did not. And he did not report the incident to police for 10 hours.

The inquest concluded that Kennedy had lied when he said he was giving Kopechne a ride home. It also ruled that his "negligent driving" appeared to have contributed to her death. Kennedy entered a guilty plea to leaving the scene of an accident and received a two-month suspended sentence. But it would be truer to say he was sentenced to life under the cloud of Chappaquiddick. He stayed on the sidelines of presidential politics, until in 1980 he tried to oust a sitting President of his own party, Jimmy Carter. He failed—and that liberated him. With the White House off the table, he concentrated on legislating. In the '80s, he teamed with conservative Utah Republican Senator Orrin Hatch to pass major legislation to address the AIDS crisis. But when Ronald Reagan tried to put Robert Bork on the Supreme Court, it was Kennedy who led the ferocious, successful liberal opposition.

In later years, stability and success

In 1991 Kennedy endured one of the messiest episodes in his public life, when he went barhopping with nephew William Kennedy Smith on the night Smith was later accused of raping a young woman. The image of the capering Senator at play reawakened all the old misgivings about Kennedy, women and alcohol.

Kennedy pulled himself back from that brink. In the summer of the same year, he began dating Victoria Reggie, a 37-year-old lawyer and gun-safety advocate who had briefly been an intern in his Senate office. They married in 1992. The union transformed Kennedy, giving him a feeling of contentment and stability he had not enjoyed for years. Newly energized, the legislator moved on to such accomplishments as supervising the passage of the Family and Medical Leave Act. Later, he joined GOP President George W. Bush to pass the No Child Left Behind Act. But in 2002, Kennedy was one of the 23 Senators who voted against authorizing the Iraq war. Years later, he would call it the "best vote" he ever cast in the Senate.

By that time, there had been a lot of good votes—votes that left the country a changed place and a better one. Granted more time than his brothers, Ted took the family mythology and shaped it into something real and enduring. Upon his Inauguration in 1961, John Kennedy gave Ted, the last born of the Kennedy siblings, an engraved cigarette box. It read, "And the last shall be first." That was almost 50 years ago. Neither of them knew then in just what ways that prophecy might turn out to be true.

—By Richard Lacayo

Edward Kennedy. Challenge, reversal and achievement

TOP ROW, LEFT TO RIGHT: BACHRACH—GETTY IMAGES; POPPERFOTO—GETTY IMAGES. SECOND ROW: JOHN LOENGARD—TIME LIFE PICTURES. THIRD ROW: JOHN LOENGARD—TIME LIFE PICTURES; RON EDMONDS—AP IMAGES. FOURTH ROW: BROOKS KRAFT—CORBIS; JOHN MOTTERN—AFP/GETTY IMAGES

Great Expectations

The story of the Kennedys is one of the great family sagas of U.S. politics. Joe Kennedy dreamed that one of his four boys would become President, and after Joe Jr. died in World War II, second son Jack picked up the torch and won the White House in 1960. Yet by mid-1968 both Jack and Bobby had been assassinated, and only Ted survived. But his chances at the presidency were shattered by the Chappaquiddick incident in 1969. At left, he appears for a hearing.

At His Side

Ted married Joan Bennett, near right, in 1958. Over the next nine years, they had three children: Kara, Edward Jr. and Patrick. But by 1982, the combination of her prolonged struggle with alcohol and his infidelities led them to divorce. His 1992 marriage to Victoria Reggie, far right, helped pave the way to the successes of his later years.

Final Days

Kennedy's endorsement of Barack Obama early in the 2008 primary race was a powerful boost to the Illinois Senator's candidacy; at left the two men appear with Caroline Kennedy Schlossberg. After learning he had brain cancer in May 2008, Kennedy spent much of his time sailing and writing his memoirs.

49

Somber Journey. A reunion at Arlington

Ted Kennedy was granted a blessing denied his three older brothers: the chance to live a long life, see his grandchildren grow, and, as Ted said in 1999, eulogizing his young nephew John F. Kennedy Jr., "to comb gray hair." After he was diagnosed with brain cancer in 2008, Kennedy had time to put his affairs in order, write his memoir *True Compass* (published in September 2009) and reminisce with friends and family.

Kennedy succumbed to the disease on Aug. 25 at his home in Hyannis Port, Mass., and during the weekend of Aug. 28-30, Americans watched as the last of the Kennedy brothers was laid to rest. On Friday, Kennedy's body lay in state at the John F. Kennedy Presidential Library in Boston, Mass. That night, close friends and family gathered for an old-fashioned Irish wake, as familiar songs were sung and good times

recalled by friends both personal and political, including Republican Senators Orrin Hatch and John McCain. On Saturday morning, a funeral Mass was held at Boston's Our Lady of Perpetual Help Basilica. President Obama delivered the eulogy, describing Kennedy as "the heir to a weighty legacy, a champion for those who had none, the soul of the Democratic Party and the lion of the U.S. Senate." Kennedy's two sons, Edward Jr. and Patrick, also offered moving reminiscences of their father.

Following the funeral, Senator Kennedy's casket was flown to Washington. His funeral cortege stopped briefly at the U.S. Capitol, where hundreds of his former staffers had assembled to honor his memory. As twilight fell at Arlington National Cemetery, Kennedy was interred close by the resting places of his two older brothers.

Hail and farewell
At right, some 50,000 people filed by the Senator's casket at the John F. Kennedy Presidential Library.

On Aug. 29, staff members gathered at the U.S. Capitol as the cortege stopped for a salute, below, before Kennedy was laid to rest at Arlington, bottom right.

LEFT: RICKY CARIOTO—POOL/GETTY IMAGES; RIGHT, TOP: EMMANUEL DUNAND—AFP/GETTY IMAGES; RIGHT, BOTTOM: DOUG MILLS—THE NEW YORK TIMES/REDUX PICTURES

In Brief

ESSENTIAL STORIES

Wildfires

'TIS THE SEASON *The big fires keep coming, and Californians keep fighting them. The most devastating blaze of 2009 was the Station Fire, which began in August north of Los Angeles; above, firefighters have set a backfire to keep the main blaze from devouring homes in La Crescenta on Sept. 1. The flames burned across some 251 sq. mi. and killed two firefighters. Earlier in the summer, the La Brea Fire burned some 136 sq. mi. outside Santa Barbara.*

Terror
A Major Plot Foiled

In what federal authorities said was one of the most plausible terror plans associated with al-Qaeda yet discovered, Colorado resident Najibullah Zazi, 24, was arrested on Sept. 19 by the FBI, along with his father, New York City taxi driver Mohammed Wali Zazi, 53, and a Queens, N.Y., imam, Ahmad Afzali, 37. On Sept. 24 Zazi was indicted on terrorism-conspiracy charges; he later pleaded not guilty.

Authorities said Zazi had flown from Newark, N.J., to Peshawar, Pakistan, on Aug. 28, 2008, where they believe he attended terror training camps run by al-Qaeda. Zazi, they said, had marching orders, accomplices and the willpower to deliver a stunning blow. He had purchased chemicals that could be used to make bombs, and is believed to have

"cooked" them in a rented apartment outside Denver. His laptop computer contained notes on building bombs.

Zazi was born in Pakistan but came to the U.S. after his father immigrated to New York City. Zazi was radicalized after the 9/11 terror attacks; in 2006 he began traveling to Pakistan, where he married and fathered two children. He moved to Aurora, Colo., a Denver suburb, early in 2009; he was arrested there after he visited New York City, where authorities say he hoped to stage a major attack. In the same week Zazi was arrested, the FBI also snared two alleged, if less well prepared, lone-wolf terrorists in Texas and Illinois.

Floods
Swamped In Georgia

Torrential September rains caused major floods throughout Georgia, with the capital city of Atlanta and its suburbs especially hard hit. Eight lives were lost, including that of an infant who was torn from his father's arms by raging floodwaters, and thousands of homes were inundated. Governor Sonny Perdue cited 17 counties to be in a

state of emergency, and President Obama declared the region a disaster area, qualifying it for federal aid.

Above, streets in Austell, Ga., on the outskirts of Atlanta, are seen heavily flooded on Sept. 22.

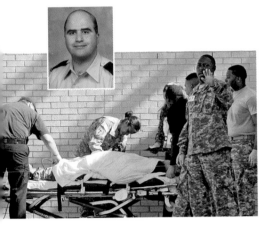

Tragedies

Massacre at Fort Hood

Major Nidal Malik Hasan, 39, a U.S. Army psychiatrist, killed 13 soldiers and injured 30 others when he opened fire in a processing facility at the Fort Hood military base in Texas on Nov. 5. Hasan, a Muslim, was said to oppose U.S. policy in the Middle East and was due to be deployed to Afghanistan.

Exposés

A Video Sting Fells ACORN

The urban activists at the Association of Community Organizations for Reform Now (ACORN) have been under fire for years. But after journalists James O'Keefe and Hannah Giles released videos in which they posed as a pimp and a prostitute and ACORN workers, below, were seen counseling them on how to operate underage prostitution rings and avoid taxes and immigration laws, Congress voted to cut off all funding for the group.

Crime

Murders, Victims, and a Kidnapping Solved

AFTER 18 YEARS, KIDNAP VICTIM JAYCEE LEE DUGARD IS FOUND

In a case so bizarre as to rival such tales as *The Silence of the Lambs*, authorities located Jaycee Lee Dugard, top right, who was kidnapped at age 11 from a school bus stop in South Lake Tahoe, Calif., on June 10, 1991. Phillip Craig Garrido, 58, bottom right, and his wife Nancy Garrido, 54, were arrested and charged with the kidnapping. Authorities said the two had held Dugard in a ramshackle group of tents in the backyard of their home in Antioch, Calif., since the kidnapping, and that Garrido had fathered two daughters by Dugard; they were ages 11 and 15 at the time of the discovery. Garrido had served two terms in federal prisons, for sexual assault in the 1970s and for violating his parole for marijuana possession in the 1990s. After neighbors voiced concerns, local police had visited the Garrido property before but failed to check the backyard.

CRAIGSLIST MURDER

Massachusetts police arrested Philip Markoff, 23, on April 20 and charged him with armed robbery, kidnaping and murder in two cases involving women he had met via the online ad service Craigslist; one was killed. Markoff pleaded not guilty. Rhode Island police say he is a suspect in an assault case.

HOLOCAUST MUSEUM

James Wenneker von Brunn, 89, was charged with the murder of security guard Stephen Johns at the U.S. Holocaust Memorial Museum in Washington, D.C. on June 10. Von Brunn, a Holocaust denier who ran a white supremacist website, was convicted of attempting to kidnap Federal Reserve officials in 1981.

YALE MURDER

On Sept. 17 police in Connecticut arrested Raymond Clark III, 24, and he was charged with the murder of Annie Le, 24, a Yale University doctoral candidate. Both Le and Clark worked in a Yale medical lab where her body was found stuffed inside a wall on Sept. 13— the day she was to be married.

World

▢ The year's most surprising story emerged in theocratic Iran, as angry voters took to the streets by the tens of thousands to oppose the results of an election they declared to be fixed. With U.S. forces in Iraq standing down, attention turned to Afghanistan, as diplomats and generals debated the purpose, extent and length of the growing U.S. commitment to a long-troubled land. Meanwhile, Israelis and Palestinians were frozen in a defiant face-off, and Libya's Muammar Gaddafi, Iran's Mahmoud Ahmadinejad and North Korea's Kim Jong Il remained atop the rogue's gallery of global despots.

Digging in *Israelis break ground for a settlement in the occupied West Bank. The U.S. called on Israel to halt such building, with no success*

Upheaval in Iran

Protesting a rigged election, irate citizens take to
the streets to challenge their theocratic regime

THE OLD SAYING ASSERTS THAT IT'S GOOD TO
be king. But in mullah-led Iran, it's even better to be Supreme Leader—the cleric who
wields the real power in the nation, with
control over the military, the judiciary, foreign policy and the nuclear program. Like his predecessors, reigning Supreme Leader Ayatullah Ali Khamenei
pays lip service to democracy by staging national elections every four years. When those elections were held,
on June 12, few doubted that the regime's candidate,
hard-line incumbent President Mahmoud Ahmadinejad, would prevail against his three opponents. Sure
enough, on June 13 Khamenei prematurely certified
Ahmadinejad the winner in a landslide—a result TIME
analyst Joe Klein, on the scene, called "phantasmic."

Yet if the result was predictable, what followed was
not: Iranians by the tens of thousands took to the streets
of capital city Tehran to protest the result, in the largest and most public challenge to Iran's rulers since Islamic clerics took control of the nation in the revolution of 1979 led by Ayatullah Khomeini. Day after day,
protesters wearing green, the color associated with the
campaign of runner-up Mir-Hossein Mousavi, marched
through the streets—men and women, old but more often young—denouncing the result and defying the regime's calls to desist. And night after night, the last call
of the muezzin was followed by shouts of "Death to the
dictator!" from the city's roofs and balconies.

The regime soon struck back, sending in its thugs—
the Basij, a paramilitary group 6 million strong—to bash
heads and restore order. By the end of June, the demonstrations had fizzled out, but they reignited on July 30,
when thousands turned out to commemorate the death
of Neda Agha-Soltan, the movement's martyr. The regime
had put a cork in the bottle, while its foes lacked a clear
long-term goal. But few believed that the surprisingly vocal opposition movement had been silenced for good. "It's
the national duty of every single man and woman to go to
the streets," a university student protester in her mid-20s
told TIME in August. "This is far from over."

Outrage *A demonstrator states his case at a June 16 protest rally. At top left, foes Ahmadinejad and Mousavi*

The popular revolt *Runner-up Mir-Hossein Mousavi, then 67, who came to embody resistance to the regime, waves to his supporters at a June 15 rall*

n Tehran, two days after Supreme Leader Ayatullah Ali Khamenei declared Mahmoud Ahmadinejad the election victor in a landslide

The Fire This Time

At top, anti-regime protesters gather around a car they set afire after hearing reports that a fellow demonstrator had been shot in Tehran on June 15. The regime attempted to block most forms of communication, but sympathizers worldwide tracked the protests via Twitter feeds.

Before: A Hand for Ahmadinejad

Above, at a political rally on June 10, two days before the election, a woman's hand has been painted with the Iranian flag, showing her allegiance to the ruling regime and its candidate, Ahmadinejad.

After: Hail to the Hero

An Ahmadinejad supporter holds a banner aloft in celebration on June 14, one day after the surprisingly early announcement that the regime's candidate had won the election with 63% of the vote. He was sworn in for a second term on Aug. 5, amid further protests.

A Demand for Democracy

Iranian citizens residing in Syria cast their votes in the national election at the Iranian embassy in Damascus on June 12, top. When the landslide victory for Ahmadinejad was announced, Iranian Americans in a number of U.S. cities staged protest marches in sympathy with their countrymen. The U.S. took a low profile during the protests, as President Barack Obama declared he did not want to offer Iran's regime a chance to accuse the U.S. of meddling.

Silent Voices

Women were a strong presence in the protest marches; these chador-clad Mousavi supporters wear green tape over their mouths to show that their votes were not counted. "They cannot turn this nation into a prison of 70 million people," said Mousavi on July 29, as authorities continued to round up protesters, and allegations emerged that the regime's foes were being raped and abused in prisons.

SPOTLIGHT

Neda. Face of the Opposition

Revolutions thrive on the blood of martyrs, and for protesters in Iran, Neda Agha-Soltan, 26, who was shot in the chest while walking to a demonstration on June 20, became an icon. A bystander with a camera captured her death on video, and the moving footage, below, quickly traveled around the world. Onlookers described a Basiji militiaman on a motorcycle as her murderer.

Agha-Soltan was one of the middle-class, educated young people who are increasingly challenging the mullah-led Iranian regime. An aspiring singer and musician who worked in her family's travel agency, she was widely traveled and had not been heavily involved in politics before the election. The name Neda means "voice" or "divine message" in Farsi, and Neda was quickly hailed as the "Voice of Iran."

In Shi'ite observances, the 40-day anniversary of a person's death is an occasion for renewed mourning. On July 30, 40 days after Neda's death, Tehran's streets again filled with protesters. Security forces were spread too thin and could not quell the crowds in many neighborhoods, TIME reported, and protesters began chanting "Death to Khamenei," a name almost no one dared utter in previous protests.

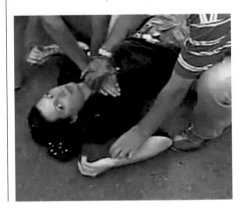

Power Of the People

A TIME correspondent's eyewitness account of Iran's postelection turmoil

BY NAHID SIAMDOUST/TEHRAN

WHEN A MILLION PEOPLE SHOWED UP ON REV-olution Avenue in downtown Tehran to protest the results of the June 12 presidential election, most of them wore sneakers, in case they had to run for their lives. The crowd included people of all walks and ages. Students holding posters that read LIES FORBIDDEN walked side by side with chadori house-wives, heavily made-up young girls, manual laborers, middle-aged government workers and the elderly. The marchers didn't chant insulting slogans, and there were few police in sight. Beneath the placid surface simmered frustration and anger—but also traces of hope. "People have come out because they've finally had enough. They're tired of all the lies that [President Mahmoud] Ahmadinejad has dished out," said Mas-soumeh, 46, who brought her two young daughters to the march. (Like most other Iranians I talked to, she did not want to give her full name.)

The popular revolt that spread across the country in the days after the election has been as startling to ordi-nary Iranians as to the authorities trying to suppress it. Not since the Islamic revolution of 1979 has Tehran seen such spontaneous outpourings of emotion. With-in hours of the announcement of the election results, Tehranis developed their own sign language of dissent.

People passing one another stretched hands in peace signs. Drivers on jam-packed streets honked their horns in protest. Apartment dwellers climbed to their rooftops to shout *"Allahu akbar"* and "Death to dictator!"—a gesture last seen three decades ago. When the regime blocked the Internet and cell-phone net-works, protesters organized rallies by word of mouth. It was democracy in action. "The amazing thing is that this movement has no leader," said Sima, 40, a book editor in Tehran. "Sure, people support [opposition presidential candidate Mir-Hossein] Mousavi, but the real reason they're here is to protest against the fraud."

It's not yet clear where the movement is headed. The regime has crushed challenges to its authority before, most recently in 1999, when students poured into the streets to protest the closing of a reformist newspa-per, prompting the government to unleash vigilantes on them. The state deployed its shock troops again this time: members of the Basij, a pro-Ahmadinejad paramilitary group, stormed dormitories at Tehran University, reportedly killing five students and detain-ing hundreds. At least one demonstrator was killed when a Basiji opened fire on a crowd. There are eyewit-ness reports of deaths from clashes across Iran. Yet no matter what transpires—whether the government bows to the demands for change or launches a bloodier crackdown—Iran will never be the same. The election and its aftermath exposed the cynicism of the coun-try's leaders but also revealed the determination of millions of Iranians to reach for a future that suddenly seemed within their grasp.

The mood on the streets of Tehran has been a mix of anger, exhilaration and dread. The day after Ahmadine-jad was declared the election victor in a landslide, peo-ple emptied into the streets in rage. Downtown, groups

The popular revolt … has been as startling to ordinary Iranians as to the authorities

Rise up! *Protesters gather at Tehran's Azadi Square on June 15. At right is a memorial to the 1980s Iran-Iraq war*

of demonstrators set several buses, a building and hundreds of garbage bins on fire, smashed the windows of state banks and destroyed ATMs. On Ghaem-Magham Street, I watched a lone woman dressed in a head-to-toe black chador standing on the side of the road, flashing the peace sign to passing cars and yelling, "Only Mousavi!" The woman, a 36-year-old bank employee named Maryam, had told her children to find dinner for themselves. "What I'm doing here is more important for their future," she said. When people driving by warned her that she might get beaten for speaking so openly, she said, "Let them beat me. My country is going to waste. What am I worth in comparison?"

Just then, a Basiji charged at her from nowhere carrying a metal rod. As he prepared to strike her, a group of men got out of their cars, tackled the man and started beating him. Maryam got up from the ground, composed herself and went right back to her spot to continue her mission. I watched as seven more people joined her, until they were chased away by police special forces wielding batons.

Despite the initial postelection mayhem, the government had some reason to believe that the fury would subside. Since Ahmadinejad's victory in 2005,

when many voters stayed away from the polls, the reform movement had been largely dormant. So when Mousavi called for a demonstration on June 15, no one was sure how many people would show up—until Ahmadinejad's victory speech, in which he compared the protesters to fans upset about losing a soccer match and called them a minority of "twigs and mote." A number of people I talked to at the pro-Mousavi march on Revolution Avenue cited the President's comments as reason to keep up the fight. "What he said drove me crazy," said a 26-year-old mechanic from Hashemiye, in south Tehran.

That people are now willing to risk their lives and take action shows that Iran has crossed a threshold. The nature of the demonstrations has reminded the state that people do, after all, care as much about democratic rights as they do about the economy. Ahmadinejad has done poorly on both counts, but as long as the state respected the vote, Iranians were willing to overlook other shortcomings. Now that trust is gone. "This time they went too far," says Mohsen, a 32-year-old government employee. "We already deposed one of the strongest dictatorships in the world, 30 years ago. They should know that we won't tolerate another."

An Uphill Battle

Facing a historic crossroads in Afghanistan, America's new
leaders weigh the future of the U.S. mission in the region

AFTER HE LAUNCHED THE U.S. INTO A WAR
in Afghanistan in 2001, only four weeks
after the 9/11 terrorist strikes against
America, President George W. Bush con-
ceded in a press conference he didn't
know when the conflict would end. "People often ask
me, 'How long will this last?'" he said, 96 hours after the
invasion began. "It may happen tomorrow, it may happen a month from now, it may take a year or two, but we

will prevail." Three weeks into the war, New York *Times*
reporter R.W. Apple wrote that "the ominous word quagmire has begun to haunt conversations" in Washington
about the conflict. Defense Secretary Don Rumsfeld had
little time for such grousing. "I must say that I hear some
impatience from the people who have to produce news
every 15 minutes," he said as the first month's fighting
neared its end, "but not from the American people."

Eight years later, Bush is no longer President, Rums-

On patrol *Members of the U.S. Army's 3rd Squadron 71st Cavalry Regiment patrol Afghanistan's east-central Logar Province on July 13. In March, President Obama decided to send 21,000 more troops to the nation and he installed a new top general, Stanley McChrystal, in May. By late summer there were 62,000 U.S. troops in Afghanistan—yet McChrystal told the President he would need at least 10,000 more troops if the U.S. were to prevail against Taliban insurgents*

feld no longer Defense Secretary, R.W. Apple is dead—and so are nearly 900 U.S. troops in Afghanistan, 239 of whom were killed from January through early October in 2009 alone. And most Americans have run out of patience with the war, modestly begun to overthrow the Taliban regime that had harbored Osama bin Laden and other al-Qaeda operatives before 9/11. That goal seemed to have been achieved in November 2001, when the Taliban were driven from Kabul. But the U.S. and its allies have waged an inconclusive war against the Taliban and their al-Qaeda allies ever since.

"President Obama inherited a disaster, a war which had been underresourced horribly for at least six of the last seven and a half years," former CIA official Bruce Rie-del, who was tapped by the White House to review U.S. policy in Afghanistan, said in August 2009. True enough, but Afghanistan is Obama's war now, so branded after he approved dispatching 21,000 more U.S. troops into battle in March 2009, a move that would raise the U.S. troop level there to 68,000 by year's end. He also tapped Army General Stanley McChrystal as his new Afghan commander, replacing General David McKiernan, and charged him with developing a new strategy to win the war. But McChrystal found the security situation there in a dangerous decline, and in September he asked the President to send 40,000 more U.S. troops to Afghanistan. (That number became the focus of the debate that ensued, but as TIME's Joe Klein reported in October, the general actually

Disputed Election. A victory—for fraud

The U.S. had great expectations for the Aug. 20 national election in Afghanistan: the balloting, it was hoped, would legitimize the nation's nascent democracy, enhance political stability and give the U.S. an Afghan-approved partner in Kabul. But the election proved a major disappointment: as former U.N. official Peter W. Galbraith wrote in TIME in October, "No one will ever know how many Afghans voted ... In some provinces, many more votes were counted than were cast. E.U. election monitors characterize 1.5 million votes as suspect, which would include up to one-third of the votes cast for incumbent President Hamid Karzai." Galbraith detailed a host of ways in which Karzai's government had rigged the election against chief opponent Abdullah Abdullah, a physician who had served as the nation's Minister of Foreign Affairs from 2002-06. Galbraith estimated as many as many as 1,500 of 7,000 polling places were unmonitored and had been used to file false results. The sham election was a major blow to U.S. goals in the region, inviting Americans to wonder why their troops were dying to support an undemocratic regime.

The U.S. and its allies put intense pressure on Karzai, and on Oct. 21, he agreed to accept a revised count approved by the U.N., which put his total at 48%, a number that triggered a run-off election with Abdullah. That vote was hastily scheduled for Nov. 7, but on Nov. 1, Abdullah declared that he would not participate in the runoff balloting, in effect handing the election to Karzai. On Nov. 2 the nation's Independent Election Commission declared Karzai the winner.

At risk *Specialist Codey Johnson weeps over injured comrade Specialist T.J. Fecteau, wounded by an improvised bomb on Sept. 8 in the Tangi Valley outside Afghanistan's capital, Kabul*

submitted three options for a build-up to the President, at levels of 10,000, 25,000 and 40,000 troops.)

The general's request came as the Administration was beginning a strategic review of U.S. policy in Afghanistan—and even as polls showed that fewer than 1 in 3 Americans supported an enhanced U.S. presence there. The review was one of the most wide-ranging and potentially historic debates over diplomatic and military strategy in recent history, with the stakes very high. Some critics accused the President of dithering, but Washington was haunted by the self-critical words of the architect of America's failed intervention in Vietnam, Robert McNamara, the former Secretary of Defense who died in 2009. The U.S. government, he recalled, never engaged in an honest debate over the goals of the U.S. commitment in Vietnam. "It seems beyond understanding, incredible, that we did not force ourselves to confront such issues head-on," he wrote.

More questions than answers

This time there was a head-on debate, and the situation on the ground was so complex that both those who supported an increased U.S. troop commitment to the war and those who opposed it were able to marshal compelling arguments for their point of view. The array of unknown factors in Afghanistan ranged from the military to the social to the political. Was the government of Hamid Karzai the stable, honest partner the U.S. needed to build long-term stability and unite Afghanistan's historically factious tribes? Karzai's credibility was badly undermined when the Aug. 20 national election depict-

Double-secret ballot *A burqa-clad Afghan woman votes in a Kabul mosque on Aug. 20*

ed as essential to building a strong partner for the U.S. in Kabul was so fraudulent as to call for a do-over. "If we don't have a government we can point to that has some basis of legitimacy in the country, the best generals, the best strategy, isn't going to help turn it around," said Riedel.

Was the Taliban, whose power in Afghanistan has surged in recent years, now a loose alliance of nationalists brought together by opposition to the U.S. intervention—or was it essentially the same harshly fundamentalist group that had provided the safe haven from which al-Qaeda launched the 9/11 attacks? Was the dire threat posed by a nuclear-armed, unstable Pakistan a powerful argument for keeping thousands of U.S. troops in the region? Would sending more U.S. troops into Afghanistan turn into a replay of the quagmire of Vietnam, or would it lead to stability, as did the 2007 U.S. surge in Iraq?

Counterinsurgency or counterterrorism?

The strategic review centered on two very different military strategies. One option: a counterinsurgency strategy aimed at routing the Taliban, which critics warned could amount to miring the U.S. in a potentially lengthy nation-building effort. The other: a counterterrorism approach in which the U.S. would gradually withdraw into protecting key cities and fight al-Qaeda terrorists mostly with drones and special forces. Critics of that strategy said it would amount to an admission of defeat, could open the door to new terrorist attacks and might lead to a replay of the late 1990s, when the Taliban imposed medieval codes of law on the nation, especially its women. But supporters said the counterterrorism option had become much more viable in 2009, after a vastly improved U.S. capability to gather intelligence on al-Qaeda resulted in the deaths of more than half of the 20 al-Qaeda leaders targeted to be killed. Vice President Joe Biden was said to be a key voice for the counterterrorism approach, while Senator John McCain and former V.P. Dick Cheney were among those urging the President to go "all in" in an effort to rout the Taliban.

In early November the controversial Karzai backed into an election victory after his opponent Abdullah Abdullah withdrew from a planned runoff vote. The surprising turn of events left Karzai in control, with Western allies wondering if he could put together a plausible government, newly committed to reform. As this book went to press, the U.S. government was still reviewing its strategy for the future.

Pakistan. A dangerous, unruly neighbor

U.S. strategy in Afghanistan cannot be discussed in isolation, for neighboring Pakistan casts a looming shadow over the long mountainous border that separates the two. Pakistan is the world's second-largest Islamic nation, with 180 million citizens. It has nuclear arms; a weak, unstable government led by Asif Ali Zardari, the widower of assassinated leader Benazir Bhutto; and a growing number of Islamic extremist groups, whose wrath—when not directed at India—is focused on the U.S.

The remote location and largely ungoverned nature of Pakistan's border region, South Waziristan, have made it the ideal hiding place for foreign militants, for al-Qaeda and for Afghan Taliban who fled the U.S. invasion of Afghanistan in 2001. It is also home to Tehrik-i-Taliban Pakistan, an umbrella group of militants that Pakistani officials say has been behind some 80% of terrorist attacks in the country over the past few years, including the 2007 assassination of Bhutto and the spate of violence that took 150 lives in the early fall of 2009. On Oct. 18 the government, in a long-anticipated offensive, sent some 28,000 soldiers into a remote corner of South Waziristan, in a three-pronged attack intended to trap the estimated 7,000 to 10,000 militants in the region, including some 1,000 Uzbek and foreign fighters who are thought to be affiliated with al-Qaeda. A successful campaign would be a major blow against Islamic extremism.

Aftermath *Rescuers care for the injured after a May 27 car-bomb blast in Lahore*

All yours *The U.S. placed Baghdad's Camp Rustamiyah in Iraqi hands on March 31. All such handovers were completed by June 30*

Four Days in Baghdad

As the U.S. begins winding down its mission in Iraq, the burden falls on Prime Minister Nouri al-Maliki to unite his divided land

WHEN TALK TURNS TO THE U.S. MISSION IN IRAQ, which passed its sixth anniversary in March 2009, few speak with the authority of General David Petraeus, commander of all U.S. forces in the Middle East and champion of the 2007 troop surge that helped stabilize Iraq. Looking ahead on June 29, Petraeus said, "There will be challenges. There are many difficult political issues, social issues, governmental development issues." Indeed, for Iraqis, 2009 was yet another year when every stride forward was achieved in spite of forces that threatened to drag the nation back into the chaos of its recent past. The fragile state of Iraq's current stability and of U.S. hopes to withdraw most of its fighting troops from the region by August 2010 were summed up on four very different days in 2009.

June 30 was the most festive of the four, as Iraqis celebrated the transfer of authority for security from U.S. forces into their hands, in compliance with the Status of Forces Agreement. Concluded late in 2008 between the Iraqi government and the Bush Administration, it requires that U.S. troops be out of Iraq's urban areas by June 30, 2009, and withdrawn from the country altogether by the end of 2011. Prime Minister Nouri al-Maliki's government held a massive celebration, marking the redeployment as National Sovereignty Day.

The holiday was for show: most U.S. forces had left Iraq's cities weeks before and were corralled into large rural bases. But they had stayed on patrol in the two largest cities plagued by violence, Baghdad and Mosul, as the transfer date drew near. Residents of Baghdad had been anticipating the day when they would no longer see U.S. troops rumbling along their capital's broad boulevards in heavy armored vehicles, a painful reminder of Iraq's dependency on foreigners for its security.

As expected, the U.S. withdrawal was tested both before and after June 30. More than 250 people were killed in terrorist attacks in the 10 days before the transfer of security. And the uptick of violence continued through the summer, culminating on Aug. 19—the second of the four red-letter days—when a series of explosions rocked the capital, including an enormous blast in front of the Foreign Ministry, which lies close to the Green Zone, headquarters for U.S. forces in Iraq; another exploded at the Finance Ministry. More than 80 people were killed and at least 300 injured. Just as life returned to normal, Baghdad was rocked by another pair of suicide car bombings on Oct. 25 that devastated three government buildings, killing at least 155 people and wounding 500. Both U.S. and Iraqi authorities warned that the violent attacks would continue, even accelerate, as the nation approached a critical January 2010 general election.

A reminder of that election's importance, and that Iraq's political issues are as unresolved as its security problems, came on July 31, the fourth of the year's critical days, when Parliament failed to pass a proposed British-Iraqi security agreement that would have kept Britain's navy on patrol in Iraq's gulf waters. As a result, the oil-export terminals near Basra remain vulnerable—and they facilitate more than 70% of state revenue. The larger issue: Iraq's legislators still can't agree on how to divide future oil revenues among the nation's rival

8/31/2010
The date for all U.S. combat troops to leave Iraq—if all goes well. All other U.S. troops are due to come home by Dec. 31, 2011

groups. The divisions revealed that Prime Minister al-Maliki—the Shi'ite politician who has proved over the past 3 years to be surprisingly crafty and tenacious—has still failed to forge a united nation out of Iraq's factious Shi'ites, Sunnis and Kurds. The key factor driving political violence in Iraq is the conflict over the post-Saddam distribution of power among these ancient enemies. Until it is resolved, Iraq will not find peace.

In September, al-Maliki, 59, announced that he would run in the January election under the banner of a new "State of Law" party, a national unity slate composed of Sunnis who have turned on al-Qaeda, independent politicians, tribal leaders, religious minorities and fellow members of al-Maliki's Shi'ite Dawa Party. The months before the 2010 election will be critical for him, for though Iraq may have begun as George W. Bush's war, for better or worse, ownership of it has now passed not to Barack Obama but to Nouri al-Maliki.

Déjà vu *Weeks of increasing violence followed the handover from the U.S. to Iraq of security authority in major cities. At right, an Iraqi soldier surveys damage at a bombed market in Sadr City, a Shi'ite stronghold in Baghdad, on July 21. Bombers unleashed the year's deadliest volley of blasts in Baghdad on Aug. 19 and Oct. 25*

Obama on the Road. An untested President reaches out, aiming to reboot U.S. foreign policy

AKING OFFICE AT A TIME WHEN AMERICA'S IMAGE and influence abroad were at a low ebb, President Barack Obama vowed he would walk more softly in his conduct of U.S. foreign affairs. He began reaching out aggressively to both allies and adversaries, signaling that America's new stance would favor diplomacy rather than bellicosity. The new strategy drove the President's most prominent early foray into foreign affairs, a five-day trip to the Middle East in June. TIME correspondent Scott MacLeod described Obama's speech to the Muslim world from Cairo University as "the most

important address ever given by an American leader about the Middle East." Obama's message: "This cycle of suspicion and discord must end." He delivered a similar message to Turkey's Parliament in Ankara in April.

Critics at home blasted Obama's Mideast journey as an "apology tour," but the outcome of the new U.S. stance will take years to determine. Except in Norway, where a panel of five judges stunned just about everyone— including the President—by awarding him the Nobel Peace Prize for 2009. Obama joined most onlookers in saying it was far too early in his term for the honor.

Strange bedfellows *The President visits with King Abdullah at a royal residence near Riyadh during a June visit to Saudi Arabia. At right, chief of staff Rahm Emanuel, an observant Jew whose middle name is Israel, visits with Foreign Minister Saud al-Faisal*

GERALD HERBERT—AP IMAGES

Higher-ups *The President met with world leaders in July for a G-8 summit in a setting fit for the gods of Olympus—high in the Italian Alps near L'Aquila, Italy, scene of a major earthquake in April. For once, a summit meeting lived up to its metaphorical title*

Partners *Obama fist-bumps a U.S. soldier at Camp Victory in Baghdad, where he received a warm welcome in April. They are in al-Faw Palace, built by Saddam Hussein*

Samovar diplomacy *The President, bedeviled by hostile "tea parties" at home, takes part in a more sedate version at Russian Prime Minister Vladimir Putin's dacha outside Moscow in July*

Pilgrims *A veiled Secretary of State Hillary Clinton gestures to the President and adviser Valerie Jarrett outside the Sultan Hassan Mosque in Cairo on the June trip to the Middle East*

Smiles and styles *When the Obamas visited French President Nicolas Sarkozy and wife Carla Bruni for the D-day anniversary in June, fashionistas ogled the First Ladies' fashion showdown*

China's Bridge to The Future

Fighting a global recession, China invests in one of the most ambitious public works programs ever seen

GUIZHOU PROVINCE, IN SOUTHWESTERN CHINA, IS A land of striking natural beauty: fields of bright green rape surround jagged peaks, ridges slashed with limestone outcrops and plunging waterfalls. But now the region's grandest sight is man-made: the Baling River Bridge. Due to be completed early in 2010, this 1.4-mile (2.25 km) marvel of engineering is a jarringly conspicuous splash of 21st century technology amid Guizhou's farms and rice fields, which haven't changed much in thousands of years. It's as if the Golden Gate Bridge had been dropped into a bucolic Middle-earth mountainscape.

Out of place as it may appear, this is no bridge to nowhere. Soaring a quarter-mile (400 m) above the Baling River, the $216 million span will reduce travel time considerably for the stream of trucks and cars traversing a highway that connects the provincial capital, Guiyang, with the nearest big city, Kunming, the capital of neighboring Yunnan province. Far from resenting the bridge as a white elephant, the residents of nearby Guanling, a one-stoplight town where the average income is less than $150 a year, view it as crucial to economic development and improvement in their lives. "I really cannot wait for the bridge to be completed," says Yuan Bo, 25, a graphic designer who takes a two-hour bus ride every week from his home in Anshun to help in his family's Guanling restaurant.

What's good for Yuan Bo and Guanling is good for China. While the recession-racked West spent 2008-09 debating the wisdom of borrowing billions of dollars and spend-

Overpass *Farmer Wei Xinyuan plows his field in the shadow of the Baling River Bridge in the southwestern Guizhou province*

Light at the end *A construction worker walks through a tunnel leading to the Baling River Bridge. A much larger complex of bridges and tunnels is planned to link more efficiently 35 ports in China's Pearl River Delta, the cradle of the nation's economic boom*

ing it on economic stimulus, China reached into its vast financial reserves to launch one of the most ambitious and expensive public works programs ever undertaken. The Baling River Bridge is only one of hundreds of infrastructure projects—ports, airports, bridges, schools, hospitals, highways, railroads—on which China plans to spend about $450 billion over the next several years.

Looking to the West

Announced in November 2008, China's pumped-up New Deal is aimed at more than cushioning its economic fall as the global recession bites deeply into the country's manufacturing and export sectors. The new projects will make it much easier for commerce and people to move around China, hence stimulating domestic demand and reducing China's economic reliance on exports, vital as rich foreign consumers rebuild their balance sheets and international trade contracts.

For an economy like China's, which is the world's third largest but is still just a third the size of the U.S.'s, the scale of the package is staggering. Total new spend-

ing is pegged at $586 billion, about 16% of GDP. In contrast, the $787 billion stimulus package approved by the U.S. Congress early in 2009 was just 6% of GDP. While upwards of 75% of Chinese spending will go toward infrastructure, just 10% of U.S. spending will. The difference to an extent reflects the fact that the nations are at different stages of economic development: America's railroad networks were built in the 19th century (and show it), and its interstate-highway system was mainly constructed in the 1950s and '60s. But it also speaks to the sheer scale of China's ambition to modernize itself.

While the stimulus package has risks, it also affords

$586 billion
Amount of China's economic stimulus package, 16% of the nation's gross domestic product

$787 billion

Amount of the U.S. economic stimulus package, 6% of the nation's gross domestic product

China a chance to rebalance its growing wealth. One by-product of China's prolonged expansion is that coastal regions—marked by boomtowns such as Shanghai, Guangzhou, Xiamen and Tianjin, as well as their hinterlands—have grown much faster than the country's interior provinces, which have always been poorer. For years the central government has tried various policies to lift western China, without much result. The infrastructure push gives Beijing another chance to address divisive and potentially explosive wealth gaps that have grown between east and west, rich and poor.

Mountain High, Emperor Far Away

China is using the stimulus package to play catch-up on another front: the environment. Three decades of rapid, unchecked economic growth has turned many of its rivers into cesspools, its lands into wastelands and much of its air into grimy soup. Some $30.9 billion has been allocated in the stimulus plan for "environmental projects" to help clean up the mess and put the befouled country on a path to more sustainable development. The government of Jiangsu province, for example, announced a $16 billion plan to clean up Lake Tai, once famed for its beauty and abundant fish but now better known for the choking algae blooms caused by industrial runoff that have made the water undrinkable for the millions of people who depend on it. "We are not taking environmental protection as a second priority," Jiangsu Governor Luo Zhijun declared to local reporters. "For us, it is just as important as economic development."

One concern: no matter how well intentioned, China's stimulus package may provide little more than a short-lived growth blip if officials are unable to control the perennial bugbear of Chinese economic development—pervasive corruption in local and provincial governments, which make their own way far from the brilliant technocrats in Beijing.

Graft was rife in construction projects long before the current downturn.

"Public spending is already subject to considerable siphoning off and, perhaps even more critically, waste," says Andrew Wedeman, a political scientist and Chinese-corruption expert at the University of Nebraska. In the boom years, such waste mattered less, for growth was so robust. Yet if China's GDP expands slowly, corruption could dampen recovery. "What really matters is not if funds will be siphoned off or how much will be siphoned off," Wedeman says, "but rather whether the siphoning will have a clear and negative impact on the central government's efforts to restimulate the economy."

But notwithstanding the amounts that will disappear into bank accounts in Hong Kong, casinos in Macau and the gaudy houses that stud the outskirts of every Chinese city, China stands to gain more than it loses through its building campaign. The scale of its needs remains immense: the country's leaders are, after all, attempting to move more people out of dire poverty and into something like comfort in a shorter time than has ever been seen before in human history.

And so the work goes on. At the base of the $527 million Chaotianmen Bridge across the Yangtze River in Chongqing, dozens of dump trucks and backhoes were rumbling to prepare an access road to the span in the weeks before it opened in April 2009. "It's good not having to worry about finding work and getting paid," said a laborer named Yang, who was helping construct the Chongqing Grand Theater, a magnificent music and opera house being built on a river headland within sight of the bridge. "There are so many public projects going on, there will always be a place for me."

—By Simon Elegant and Austin Ramzy

Stretching *Enormous freeway interchanges are under construction in Chongqing, China's effective capital during World War II. Its population in 2009: 31 million*

A Plague of Piracy

The dramatic rescue of an American captain ends an ordeal off
the coast of Somalia, but the raids on shipping continue

TIMES HAVE BEEN GOOD IN RECENT YEARS FOR THE increasingly bold pirates who operate off the east coast of the Horn of Africa. Based in a failed state, Somalia, that cannot police them, and ranging over a wide area, the pirates have grown fat as they feast off their prey: merchant ships and oil tankers sailing under all flags. The shipping companies that own these vessels send their unarmed crews directly into harm's way—and then routinely pay exorbitant ransoms to the pirates who have grown increasingly expert at boarding and taking over the ships. The bottom line: in 2008 alone, shipping companies paid out more than $180 million in ransom to international pirates.

Yet 2009 may prove to be the year when the pirates' good fortune began to fade. The year started with a typical scene from the region: in the first week of January, U.S. Navy photographs showed a package at the end of a parachute floating gently down onto the deck of the *Sirius Star,* a captive Saudi supertanker. Inside was a ransom reported to be as much as $3 million in bank notes. A day later, the ship's owners announced that the vessel, held by Somali pirates since mid-November, had been freed and its crew members were all safe.

In a bizarre twist of fate, however, most of the pirates didn't get to enjoy their ill-gotten gains: according to an account by a Somali-based news site, the pirates were

Captives *Opposite, a pirate holds a gun at the head of a hostage aboard the French yacht* Tanit *off the coast of Somalia. The incident took place one day before U.S. Navy* SEALs *freed Captain Richard Phillips, above, of the* Maersk Alabama. *At left, the* Maersk *enters Mombasa, Kenya, after its hijacking*

"singing in colorful tone and exchanging some ridiculous words" while motoring back to shore in bad weather when one of their skiffs capsized. Five pirates are believed to have drowned; four survived but lost their booty.

Things got even hotter for the pirates a few months later. On April 8, four Somalis clambered up ropes to board the U.S.-registered *Maersk Alabama* container ship. After a dramatic series of confrontations in which both sides took prisoners, Captain Richard Phillips, 53, offered himself as a hostage to the pirates in exchange for their captured leader. It was the first time a U.S.-flagged ship had been seized by pirates. But after the Somali chief was freed, the pirates reneged on the deal and fled with Phillips in a lifeboat; their own boat had sunk as they boarded the *Maersk Alabama*. On April 10, Phillips attempted to escape but did not succeed. And when the pirates tried to steer the small lifeboat toward the Somali coast, two U.S. Navy warships that had quickly arrived on the scene—the U.S.S. *Bainbridge* and U.S.S. *Halyburton*—repeatedly cut off them off.

When the gas tanks in the lifeboat ran out, the pirates committed a serious mistake: they agreed to accept a tow from the *Bainbridge* while they awaited the conclusion of negotiations for their ransom and Phillips' release. With the lifeboat trailing close in the wake of the *Bainbridge*, U.S. Navy SEAL snipers trained their sights on the three pirates in it; President Barack Obama had given orders allowing them to fire if Phillips' life was in danger. When a pirate was seen pointing his gun at the captain's back, the snipers fired, picking off the pirates with three perfect shots. The date was April 12, Easter Sunday in the U.S., where Americans soon joined the Phillips family in cheering the captain's survival. "His courage is a model for all Americans," said a relieved Obama.

But risks from bad weather and snipers' rifles didn't seem to deter the marauders. By September, TIME reported that 2009 had brought more than 135 pirate attacks originating from the Somali coast—more than the total number for 2008—and 28 vessels had been successfully commandeered. Part of the problem was the shipping companies' insistence on keeping crews unarmed, since allowing them to carry weapons, or even hiring armed guards to protect the crafts, would butt up against the laws of dozens of nations, which do not allow merchant marine ships to dock at their ports with weapons aboard.

Following the *Maersk* hijacking, U.S. Defense Secretary Robert Gates called on international shipping companies and governments to stop paying ransoms to the pirates entirely. But in case his advice won't be heeded, the U.S. began making plans to counter future attacks. In the spring, the Marine Corps announced it would transport 1,628 TEUS—20-ft. shipping containers crammed with munitions and explosives—to a secretive U.S. naval station on the atoll of Diego Garcia in the Indian Ocean, southeast of Somalia. And in September, the Pentagon announced plans to dispatch unmanned Reaper drone aircraft to the Seychelles Islands to patrol the waters off Somalia. It remains to be seen whether the pirates, who have been unfazed by all previous attempts to control them, will fear the Reaper.

Candidate *Mousavi addresses a campaign rally in Ardebil province, northwest of Tehran, 11 days before the disputed election*

Mir-Hossein Mousavi

The figure around whom dissident Iranians rallied is more an architect than a politician. Can he design his nation's future?

THOSE UNFAMILIAR WITH IRANIAN POLITICS MIGHT suspect that Mir-Hossein Mousavi, the challenger to Iran's President Mahmoud Ahmadinejad in the nation's election turned uprising, is a firebrand and proponent of revolution, the Walesa of Tehran. But Mousavi is an unlikely rebel. The former Prime Minister, who served from 1981 to 1989, is a middle-of-the-road figure who came out of political retirement in 2009 to run for President as the candidate of Iran's pragmatic conservatives and reformists, promising greater democracy and sober economic management in Iran and improved relations with the West.

Mousavi, 68, is an architect and artist who seems more an artist-intellectual than a politician. The day before the disputed election, he met with TIME columnist Joe Klein and Tehran correspondent Nahid Siamdoust in an art-school-and-gallery complex of his own design in Tehran. The soft-spoken candidate was cautious and precise, yet at times surpris-

ingly candid. Mousavi denounced Ahmadinejad's campaign attack on his wife, the famous artist and activist Zahra Rahnavard. "I think he went beyond our societal norms, and that is why he created a current against himself," Mousavi said. "In our country, they don't insult a man's wife [to] his face." He also criticized, as he did during the campaign, Ahmadinejad's incendiary rhetoric on international issues like Israel and the Holocaust.

Can Mousavi survive the forces the election has unleashed? "Change has already started," he told TIME. "Only part of this change is about winning in the elections. The other part will continue, and there is no going back." Indeed. Now that his followers have mounted a remarkable challenge to Ahmadinejad's re-election, Mousavi represents, with his ringing accusation of election fraud and denunciation of "dictatorship," an unprecedented challenge to the status quo by the forces of reform.

Avigdor Lieberman

Israel's hard-line Foreign Minister refuses to mince words, tread lightly—or stop the builders who erect the settlements

FOR A MAN REPUTED TO BE ISRAEL'S BIGGEST LOUD-mouth, Avigdor Lieberman speaks softly. His flat, Russian-accented baritone rarely rises above a murmur. He's not a shouter. But when Lieberman talks, people listen—less because he is Israel's top diplomat than because he has a knack for saying decidedly undiplomatic things. Lieberman believes that Israel's Arab citizens, who make up nearly 20% of the population, should be forced to sign oaths of loyalty. He has advocated the death penalty for Arab members of parliament who meet with members of Hamas. He calls the Obama Administration's push to curb the building of Jewish settlements in the West Bank a "mistake." It's not the kind of language you'd expect from a Foreign Minister, but Lieberman, 51, doesn't care. "I don't like political correctness," he says with a shrug. "I say exactly what I mean, and I mean what I say."

Lieberman's hard line is the product of his past. His family moved to Israel in 1978 from the Soviet republic of Moldavia, now Moldova. His father fought in the Red Army in World War II but, like many other Soviet Jews, later spent years of forced exile in Siberia. Once in Israel, Lieberman enrolled at Hebrew University and became active in the right-wing Likud Party. In the late '80s, he and his wife moved to Nokdim, a rugged West Bank settlement where he still lives. Around that time, he met Benjamin Netanyahu, then a rising Likud star. He ran Netanyahu's first, successful campaign for Prime Minister, in 1996, and became his chief of staff. In 1999, Lieberman split from Netanyahu, forming Yisrael Beitenu, an unapologetically nationalist party that drew its support from Israel's Russian-immigrant community. The party's most explosive position is the call for all citizens to pledge allegiance to the Jewish state as a condition of the right to vote—a barely veiled challenge to the loyalty of Israeli Arabs.

Lieberman insists he supports an independent Palestinian state and says Israel is "ready to start negotiations without preconditions." But in Lieberman's view, peace doesn't mean cohabitation. "His governing idea is, Jews on one side, Arabs on the other," says a senior official. It's an appealingly simple vision but also a cynical one. Any final agreement between Arabs and Israelis will require them to share some territory—in Jerusalem, for instance—to which both can make rightful claims. Insisting on physical separation as a prerequisite for a peace deal is a safe way to ensure that one is never struck. His views may be finding acceptance in the Israeli mainstream. But they are not the way to forge a lasting peace in the Middle East.

—*By Romesh Ratnesar*

Pilgrim *Lieberman prays at the Western Wall in the old city of Jerusalem*

In Brief

ESSENTIAL STORIES

South Pacific

ATLAS SHRUGGED *A string of natural disasters struck a wide swath of South Pacific nations in September and October. Above, after Tropical Storm Ketsana unleashed torrential late-September rains, some 80% of Manila's streets were flooded, tens of thousands of Filipinos were left homeless, and more than 330 died. On Sept. 29, a 7.6-magnitude earthquake rocked Indonesia's island of Sumatra, killing more than 520—and another struck Samoa, killing more than 1,000. The resulting tsunamis inundated the Samoan islands and Tonga, extinguishing some 180 lives.*

North Korea

Freedom's Price: A Photo-Op

North Korea's Kim Jong Il, 68, is thought to have suffered a stroke in 2008, but the "Dear Leader" survived to make more mischief: he staged missile launches toward Japan in April and July. When U.S. journalists Laura Ling, 32 (top left), and Euna Lee, 36, were taken into custody after they wandered into North Korea, Kim demanded that former President Bill Clinton fly to Pyongyang to seek their freedom. A grim Clinton complied: he sat for a photo with Kim, the price for the women's welcome release.

Nations

The Leader Board

Japan saw its most radical change in leadership in decades; Germany kept its female Chancellor in power—and Italy's leader made a spectacle of himself.

JAPAN

The Democratic Party of Japan won a historic victory on Aug. 30, sending the Liberal Democratic Party out of power for only the second time in 54 years. Yukio Hatoyama, 62, became Prime Minister and will face stern economic challenges.

GERMANY

Chancellor Angela Merkel, 55, was re-elected on Sept. 27. Her Christian Democratic Union formed a ruling coalition with the Free Democratic Party, taking some 48% of the vote.

ITALY

Media magnate and President Silvio Berlusconi, 73, jested about President Obama's "suntan," and wife Veronica Lario declared she would divorce him, charging him with pursuing affairs with much younger women.

Honduras
A Coup in Central America

Honduran President Manuel Zelaya, above, was ousted in a coup led by rightist adversary Roberto Micheletti and military officers on June 28. Insisting he was still President, Zelaya stole back into Honduras on Sept. 21. The U.S. supported Zelaya, and on Oct. 30 Micheletti agreed to let the Honduran Congress decide the matter.

Libya
A Villain's Welcome

When Libyan dictator Muammar Gaddafi set up a restitution fund in 2003 for the families of the victims of the bombing of Pan Am Flight 103, which disintegrated over Lockerbie, Scotland, in 1988, killing 270—and

when former Libyan intelligence officer Abdel Basset Ali al-Megrahi was sent to Scotland to serve a life term in jail— it seemed the case was closed. But on Aug. 20, a Scottish court released al-Megrahi on the ground that he was dying, and he returned to Libya to receive a hero's welcome from Gaddafi. The U.S. and other nations denounced the decision, amid charges that Britain approved the release to protect its oil interests in Libya.

Iran
Iran's Nuclear Dreams, Nourished in Secret

When the dust settled after the Iranian election protests in June, hard-liner Mahmoud Ahmadinejad was inaugurated for another term as President, and Iran's drive to harness nuclear energy—which it claims is for peaceful use and the U.S. believes is not—again took center stage. Hopes for a breakthrough swelled after Iran agreed to meet with the U.S., China, Russia, the U.K., France and Germany in Geneva on Oct. 1 to discuss its nuclear program. It was the first time U.S. diplomats had met with their Iranian counterparts in some 30 years.

On Sept. 17, President Obama announced that the U.S. would cancel its plans to build missile bases in Poland and the Czech Republic, long a source of friction between the U.S. and Russia. President Dmitry Medvedev of Russia praised the move, suggesting his nation might be more willing to work with the U.S. and its allies to deter Iran's nuclear ambitions. Then, at a G-20 summit meeting in Pittsburgh on Sept. 24, Obama revealed that Iran had been operating a secret nuclear research center near the ancient city of Qom, below.

At the Geneva conference, Iran agreed to allow U.N. inspections at Qom and also to a plan in which it would send low-enriched uranium to Russia to create fuel rods for its medical-research reactor in Tehran, in line with the primary demand that the U.S. and its European allies have pressed since 2006: that Iran freeze and eventually give up its uranium-enrichment program in exchange for political and economic incentives. But late in October Iran reversed course, saying it would not ship its uranium to Russia; a week later the government said that decision was not final. A frustrated U.S. and its U.N. allies accused Iranians of once again employing the delaying tactics they had used in the past to block inspections of their nuclear plants.

At right, the secret nuclear facility in Qom; below, Iran fires missiles in September. On May 20 Iran successfully tested solid-fuel, medium-range missiles capable of reaching Israel and U.S. bases in the Persian Gulf

Life

▫ A long-feared nightmare became reality as the first pandemic of the 21st century swept around the world: public health officials labeled it the H1N1 virus, but most people called it the swine flu. In the sports world, aging champions Roger Federer and Tiger Woods burnished their legends yet also revealed they were beatable, while Lance Armstrong toured France again, if sans yellow jersey. In science, too, it was a year for old bones— and for ancient gold, and for breathtaking new visions of the heavens, courtesy of the venerable Hubble telescope, which was fitted with a fresh set of specs.

Precautions *A Mexico City schoolboy returns to class after the nation closed all schools in April to prevent the spread of the H1N1 virus*

The World Fights a Flu

A virus devastates Mexico and quickly makes its way around the globe, putting health-care systems on high alert worldwide

APRIL WAS THE CRUELEST MONTH OF 2009 FOR THE health of the human race as, after years of warnings, a long-feared pandemic began circulating around the world at the speed of—well, of hundreds of jetliners flying international routes. The influenza was labeled the H1N1 virus, but it quickly was dubbed the "swine flu," a term that was misleading but proved hard to shake. The good news: on its first go-round, the virus itself wasn't that hard to shake, in most cases. With the exception of certain populations—including pregnant women, children with chronic diseases and people with respiratory ailments—H1N1 often proved no worse than the seasonal flu. A few days in bed and lots of liquids, and most patients got better. And in the U.S. a quick response by alert officials—including a host of bulletins on how to fight the spread of influenza, tough talk at a presidential press conference and a tide of school closings—helped keep the lid on the flu's impact.

As of August, the World Health Organization reported that of some 160,000 laboratory-confirmed cases of H1N1 infection worldwide, only around 1,200 people had died. Mexico, where the flu is believed to have originated, was hardest hit, with so many stricken that the government shut down schools, restaurants and concert halls; the reasons the virus was more deadly in Mexico are yet to come, though some officials suggested the flu may simply have evolved into a less powerful strain as it traveled beyond Mexico to other nations. China, hit hard by the SARS virus in 2002-03, clamped down effectively this time around, and few deaths were reported.

Bullet dodged—this time. For, like most viral epidemics, H1N1 is a seasonal malady. And though the bug never developed into the killer that health offi-cials feared it might during its spring manifestation, the world remained on high alert as fall approached, when the virus was expected to get a second wind. Sure enough, TIME reported in mid-September, the bug returned sooner than expected in the U.S., long before cold weather forced people inside, where viruses like to fester, and weeks before the official start of flu season on Oct. 4. The virus gobbled up terrain, with 26 states reporting widespread flu illness on Sept. 19. "Flu season is definitely here," Dr. Anne Schuchat, an assistant surgeon general at the federal Centers for Disease Control and Prevention (CDC), told TIME. "We don't know when it is going to peak or how many waves there will be."

By the fall, however, health officials had developed a weapon against the disease: shipments of a hastily developed flu vaccine began arriving in U.S. communities in mid-October, sparking a national vaccination campaign run by state and local governments. Early tests on the vaccine were promising: there were no red flags about safety, and studies suggested that many Americans would be able to build up sufficient flu resistance with just one dose, instead of the two or three doses that were initially predicted. As federal officials prepared to launch the most ambitious mass-vaccination campaign in U.S. history, their biggest concern was rising skepticism about the safety of vaccines in general, a trend that had been gaining momentum in recent years.

But the government soon had a different problem on its hands: supplies of the vaccine were lagging badly behind earlier projections, due to manufacturing delays. In late October officials revealed that only about 28 million doses would be available by month's end, about 30 percent below the 40 million they had predicted. Almost concurrently, President Obama declared the flu outbreak a national emergency on Oct. 23, allowing local hospitals to adopt emergency protocols for treatment. The flu, said CDC officials, was widespread in 46 U.S. states. Although estimates of the total numbers of those afflicted were inexact, the government said that millions of Americans had been stricken since the outbreak began in the spring and that more than 1,000 of them had died from the disease.

"Flu season is definitely here. We don't know when it is going to peak or how many waves there will be."
—DR. ANNE SCHUCHAT, CDC, SEPT., 2009

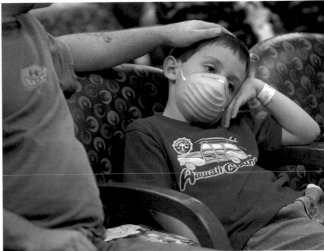

On alert *Clockwise from top left, people don masks to ward off infection in Mexico City; Fort Worth, Texas; Lanzhou, China; and Paris*

H1N1 by the Numbers. The staggering statistics of a global flu

50 MILLION

The last great global pandemic, the so-called Spanish flu of 1918, killed more than 50 million people. It began as a mild springtime flu, then returned as a highly efficient killing machine in the fall

160,000

The number of lab-certified cases of H1N1 infection reported worldwide as of August 2009. Some 1,200 deaths were reported at that time, a relatively small fraction of those afflicted

28 MILLION

Number of doses of the H1N1 vaccine on hand in the U.S. by Oct. 31. Some 10 million to 20 million more doses were expected to be added each week through year's end

6.8 BILLION

Earth's total population in 2009. Almost every human on the planet was at risk from the H1N1 virus, though residents of infrequently visited areas were less likely to contract the flu

A Long-Lost Relative

The oldest hominid skeleton ever discovered offers unexpected
clues to what our ancient ancestors may have looked like

FIGURING OUT THE STORY OF HUMAN ORIGINS IS LIKE
assembling a huge, complicated jigsaw puzzle
that has lost most of its pieces. Many will never
be found, and those that do turn up are sometimes hard
to place. Every so often, though, fossil hunters stumble
upon a discovery that fills in a big chunk of the puzzle
all at once—even as it reshapes the very picture they
thought they were building. The path of just such a discovery began in November 1994 with the unearthing
of two pieces of bone from the palm of a hominid hand
in the dusty Middle Awash region of Ethiopia. Within
weeks, more than 100 additional bone fragments were
found during an intensive search-and-reconstruction
effort that would go on for the next 15 years and culmi-
nate in a key piece of evolutionary evidence revealed in
October 2009: the 4.4 million-year-
old skeleton of a likely human ancestor known as *Ardipithecus ramidus* (abbreviated *Ar. ramidus*).

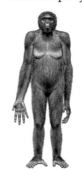

In a special issue of *Science* magazine, researchers unveiled Ardi, a
125-piece hominid skeleton that is
1.2 million years older than the celebrated Lucy *(Australopithecus afarensis)* and by far the oldest one ever
found. Tim White of the University
of California, Berkeley, a co-leader of the Middle Awash
research team that discovered and studied the new fossils, says, "To understand the biology, the parts you really want are the skull and teeth, the pelvis, the limbs
and the hands and the feet. And we have all of them."

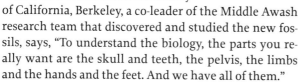

That is the beauty of Ardi—good bones. Along with
the more than 150,000 plant and animal fossils collected
nearby from the same time period, they offer rich new
clues to what the last common ancestor shared by humans and chimps might have looked like before their
lineages diverged about 7 million years ago.

Ardi is the earliest and best-documented descendant
of that common ancestor. Yet the surprising thing is
that she bears little resemblance to chimpanzees, our
closest living primate relatives. The elusive common
ancestor's bones have never been found, but scientists

previously supposed Great-Great-Grandpa looked most
nearly like a knuckle-walking, tree-swinging ape. Yet
"[Ardi is] not chimplike," according to White, which
means that the last common ancestor probably wasn't
either. "This skeleton flips our understanding of human
evolution," says Kent State University anthropologist
C. Owen Lovejoy, a member of the Middle Awash team.
"It's clear that humans are not merely a slight modifica-
tion of chimps, despite their genomic similarity."

So what does that mean? Ardi's anatomy suggests that
chimpanzees may actually have changed more than
humans have over the past 7 million years or so. That's
not to say Ardi was more humanlike than chimplike.
White describes her as an "interesting mosaic" with
certain uniquely human characteristics: bipedalism, for
one. Ardi stood 47 in. (120 cm) tall
and weighed about 110 lbs. (50 kg),
making her roughly twice as heavy
as Lucy. The structure of her upper
pelvis, leg bones and feet indicates
she walked upright on the ground,
while still able to climb. Her foot
had an opposable big toe for grasping tree limbs but lacked the flexi-
bility that apes use to grab and scale
tree trunks and vines, nor did it have
the arch that allowed *Australopithecus* to walk without
lurching from side to side. A dexterous hand, more ag-
ile than a chimp's, made her better at catching things
on the ground and carrying them while walking on two
legs. Her wrist, hand and shoulder bones show that she
wasn't a knuckle walker and didn't hang or swing ape-
style in trees. Rather, she employed a primitive method
of palm-walking typical of extinct apes.

"When we started our work [in the Middle Awash],"
says White, "the human fossil record went back to
about 3.7 million years." Now scientists have a trove
of information from an era some 700,000 years closer
to the dawn of the human lineage. The search for more
pieces goes on, but the outlines of the puzzle, at least,
are coming into focus.

—*By Michael D. Lemonick and Andrea Dorfman*

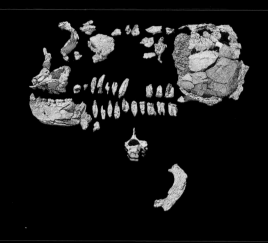

TEETH
Their size, shape, structure and enamel composition indicate Ardi was omnivorous. Males of her species lacked the daggerlike fangs of gorillas and chimps, suggesting that *Ardipithecus*, unlike them, didn't fight over mates but may instead have pair-bonded like humans.

FEET
Unlike any later hominid, Ardi had an opposable, grasping big toe that aided in climbing. The rest of her flat foot was rigid enough to act as a propulsive lever when she walked on two legs. Her gait could be somewhat clumsy, and if she ran, she would tire quickly.

PELVIS
The broad upper portion allowed the lumbar (lower back) vertebrae to curve inward, essential for upright walking. The apelike lower pelvis anchored powerful hamstring muscles used for climbing.

HANDS
Ardi didn't swing through trees much, but her long, dexterous fingers and flexible palms were ideal for grasping. Her wrists were equally flexible, enabling her to bend her hands back and "palm-walk" along branches, just as extinct apes did.

VITAL STATISTICS
Female, most likely a young adult: 47 in. (120 cm) tall; 110 lbs. (50 kg)

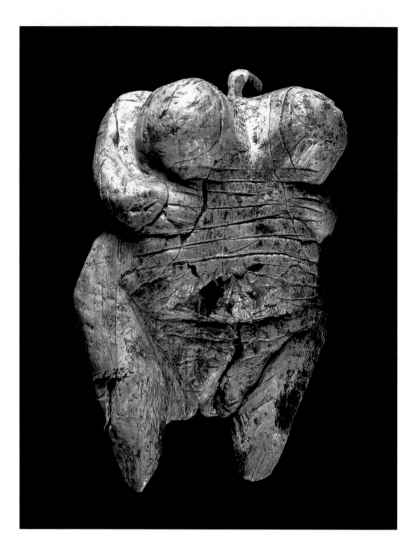

Big-boned gal *German archaeologist Nicholas Conard was the leader of the team that unearthed the ancient carving in Germany. The object was found in six pieces, with the largest fragment composing most of the out-sized torso. The sculpture is only 2.4 in. (6 cm) tall*

PROFILE

The Venus of Hohle Fels

The earliest-known representation of a human being opens a window into the world of prehistoric men and women

SCIENCE THRIVES ON REVELATIONS, AND PERHAPS the field's biggest surprise of 2009 was that the year's superstars turned out to be a pair of elderly German women. Then again, these were extremely elderly women: one was a 47 million-year-old primate fossil, and the other was the oldest representation of a human figure yet discovered, a 35,000 year-old sculpture of a naked female. The six fragments of carved mammoth ivory that form the figure were unearthed at the Hohle Fels cave in southwestern Germany in September 2008, and their discovery was announced in the science journal *Nature* in May. Scientists said they uncovered the sculpture at a depth of 3 m (more than 9 ft.) under the ground. The figure, dubbed the Venus of Hohle Fels, is similar to but older than previously discovered Paleolithic sculptures of human females, such as the well-known Venus of Willendorf, a 25,000-year-old figure found in Austria in 1908.

The Venus of Hohle Fels has exaggerated sexual characteristics and a short, squat body; most scientists believe such sculptures served as symbols of fertility. A carved ring replaces the figure's head, suggesting it was worn as a pendant. The very early date assigned to the Venus of Hohle Fels pushes back the accepted period for when early humans first began to create representations of themselves.

Ida, Primitive Primate

A 47 million-year-old critter's remains get a red carpet rollout—but the year's oldest celebrity deserved the fuss

WHEN CHARLES DARWIN AND P.T. BARNUM TEAM UP, guess who takes a backseat? From the get-go, the May 19, 2009, revelation of the 1983 discovery of a 47 million-year-old primate fossil in Germany was a master class in ballyhoo. The first breathless press releases shouted in caps: "MEDIA ALERT! WORLD-RENOWNED SCIENTISTS REVEAL A REVOLUTIONARY SCIENTIFIC FIND THAT WILL CHANGE EVERYTHING." Next up in the rigorously planned rollout of the new celebrity, dubbed Ida: an international press conference at the American Museum of Natural History in New York City, the publication of a book on the find, an ABC News exclusive and a prime-time television special on the History Channel. Whew!

Beyond the puffery, the fossil find, as described in a paper published in the online journal *PLoS One*, really is important. The young mammal, which would have looked like a cross between a lemur and a small monkey, is astonishingly complete, from the skull to the tip of the tail. There are even the remains of what was presumably Ida's final meal.

The fossil is also important because of its age. Ida dates to a period when temperatures were warmer than they are today and mammals underwent a burst of evolutionary diversification. That's when primates began splitting into two branches: the anthropoids, predecessors of monkeys, apes and humans; and the prosimians—lemurs and their kin.

Ida has some characteristics of both branches, suggesting that she could be a transitional animal that gave rise to the anthropoids and, ultimately, to us. All of which renders the claim that Ida is a "revolutionary scientific find that will change every-thing" absolutely true—as long as by "everything," you mean "whether the branch of the primate fam-ily that includes monkeys, apes and humans comes from the suborder *strepsirrhinae* or the suborder *hap-lorrhinae*," according to the *PLoS One* paper. And by "change," you mean "adds information that may or may not help settle the question, but whose implica-tions won't be known for a long time in any case."

—*By Michael Lemonick*

Cold case: A 47 million-year-old clue *Scientists christened the primate* Darwinius masillae, *but they also gave the creature a shorter, more memorable handle: Ida. The fossil was found in an abandoned quarry called the Messel Pit, near Frankfurt, Germany, in 1983, but it was held by a private collector until its discovery was announced in 2009*

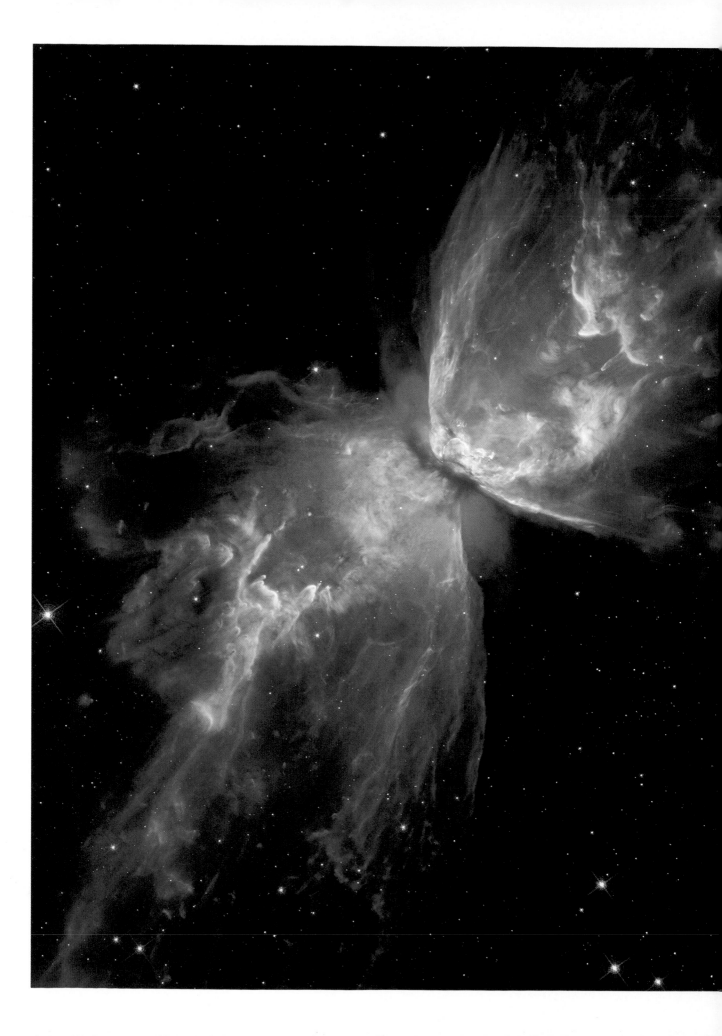

Starstruck

After a fix-up by visiting astronauts, the Hubble Space Telescope dazzles skywatchers with wondrous visions

ENTHUSIASTIC ASTRONOMERS HAVE BEEN known to describe the Hubble Space Telescope as the greatest single engine of scientific discovery ever built. That may or may not be the case, but it's undeniable that the orbiting observatory can take credit for creating some of the most compelling visions of nature ever recorded. In 2009, 19 years after it was launched, NASA's venerable eye on the skies dazzled skywatchers with a new set of images of deep space, thanks to an overhaul of its components by the seven crew members of the *Atlantis* shuttle that hooked up with Hubble in May.

In what NASA called the final mission to Hubble before it is retired, the astronauts gave the platform a thorough upgrade over the course of five spacewalks. They installed two new instruments: the Wide Field Camera 3, which will give astronomers the most powerful telescope yet devised to search for early star systems and planets orbiting other stars, and the Cosmic Origins Spectrograph, designed to study the chemical evolution of star formation. And they upgraded many of the operating systems on the platform, including its gyroscopes and specific components of Hubble's three other cameras. "It's more like brain surgery than construction," said NASA's lead flight director, Tony Ceccacci. "Hubble spacewalks are comparable to standing at an operating table, doing very dextrous work." The surgery was a success, as NASA proved when it released these stunning visions from Hubble's new eyes.

Points of light *At left is one of the most spectacular images taken by Hubble's new Wide Field Camera 3: the NGC 6302 galaxy in the Scorpius constellation, called the Butterfly Nebula. At top above is Stephan's Quintet, a grouping of galaxies in Pegasus, some 290 million light-years away. At bottom above is Omega Centauri (NGC 5139), a globular star cluster in Centaurus. Astronomers estimate some 100,000 stars are present in this picture, of the cluster's total of 10 or 12 billion*

In Brief

ESSENTIAL STORIES

Climate Change

WATER—AND COURAGE—NEEDED

WATER—AND COURAGE—NEEDED As climate change plagued the planet, Australians endured the eighth year of a devastating drought, and in China's province of Jiangxi, above, children tried to catch fish in a shrinking pond. Meanwhile scientists said the Arctic sea-ice pack had shrunk to its third-smallest size on record. Yet the world's politicians seemed unable to make the tough decisions necessary to deal with the crisis. Hopes that nations would address the problem rested on a critical U.N.-sponsored meeting on the issue, scheduled to take place in Copenhagen from Dec. 7 to 18.

Archaeology

An Amateur's Golden Find

It was a good year for the world's part-time scientists. An Australian skygazer was first to see a comet's impact with Jupiter. And Terry Herbert, 55, an unemployed treasure-hunter wielding a metal detector

in south Staffordshire, located one of the most extensive troves of Anglo-Saxon artifacts ever uncovered in Britain.

Among the more than 1,345 items that made up Herbert's haul were a checkerboard piece inlaid with garnets and a damaged golden plaque, left, that shows two birds of prey gripping a fish. The artifacts date from A.D. 675-725, when Scandinavian and German invaders vied with native tribes to control Britain. The wealth on display—totaling some 11 lbs. (.45 kg) of gold—suggested that the Angles and Saxons were much richer than historians had previously believed.

Underwater Archaeology

A Visit to *Victory*

The British warship H.M.S. *Victory*, a precursor of the famed flagship of Admiral Horatio Nelson, went down in a storm in 1744 near the Channel Islands off Britain's coast. Some 1,100 sailors, including the ship's captain, Sir John Balchin, were killed.

On Feb. 2, 2009, the famed modern-day shipwreck-finders at Odyssey Marine Exploration announced they had located the wreck and had retrieved artifacts from it. The group found *Victory*'s remains about 62 mi. (100 km) from where historians thought she had sunk.

Divers retrieved the richly wrought 42-lb. cannon at left from the wreck of H.M.S. Victory

Paleontology
A Downsized Dinosaur

What's more exciting than everyone's favorite dinosaur, *Tyrannosaurus Rex?* A pocket *T. Rex*—and that's what scientists unveiled in September 2009. Its bones, above, were uncovered in Inner Mongolia some years ago, but kept secret. The new dinosaur, *Raptorex kriegsteini*, was 9 ft. (2.7 m) long, one-fifth the size of *T. Rex*, and it flourished about 60 million years before *T. Rex* appears in textbooks—books paleontologists will now be rewriting.

Nature
On the Trail of New Species

A BBC film crew shooting a nature documentary in the extinct volcano Mount Bosavi in Papua New Guinea, discovered some 40 animal species never before known to science, it was announced in September 2009. Among the creatures new to science: a wooly vegetarian rat some 3 ft. (1 m) long, above, as well as 16 new frog species, at least three new fish species, 20 new species of insects and spiders and one new bat species.

Physics
Colliding with Reality

When scientists foul up on a major project, there's no room to hide. Remember the Hubble Space Telescope, which was launched into orbit in 1990—and was only then found to have a distorted mirror? Particle physicists at the CERN research

center in Switzerland became the latest victims of the Big Project Blues, when the Large Hadron Collider, which took 25 years to plan and $6 billion to build, broke down soon after it was first fired up in September 2008. Scientists now concede it will not operate at full power until the end of 2010—if all goes well.

Jupiter • July 23, 2009
Hubble Space Telescope
Wide Field Camera 3

NASA, ESA, H. Hammel (Space Science Institute), and the Jupiter Impact Team

Astronomy

On July 19, amateur Australian astronomer Anthony Wesley, 44 made history when he was the first to note a smudge on Jupiter. The big spot, scientists believe, was made when a comet less than 1 km (.6 mi.) in diameter smacked into the planet. Space scientists also found indications that there may be water on the moon, and that Saturn is surrounded by an enormous ring of ice and dust, far outside its familiar inner rings, that is invisible to the naked eye.

Paleontology
Supersized and Slithering

Scientists from the University of Florida and the Smithsonian Institution announced early in 2009 that they had discovered the remains of an enormous snake in Cerrejón, Colombia. Dubbed *Titanoboa cerrejonensis*, the critter was 42 ft. (13 m) long and lived some 60 million years ago. The cold-blooded reptile's large size suggested the earth's climate was hotter at that time than scientists expected.

Wasteland *Detroit was once America's fourth largest city. Today, some one-third of it, an area roughly the size of San Francisco, lies vacant, above. At left, the ruins of the Michigan Theatre, a majestic palace built in 1926 in Detroit's heyday and now used as a parking lot*

Rebooting the Motor City

It was the foremost symbol of America's can-do spirit in the 20th century. Can Detroit rise from the ashes?

DETROIT HAS BECOME AN ICON OF THE FAILED AMERICAN CITY, BUT VAST SWATHS OF IT don't look like a city at all. Turn your Chevy away from downtown and the postcard skyline gives way first to seedy dollar stores and then to desolation. The collapse of the Big Three automakers has accelerated Detroit's decline, but residents have been steadily fleeing since the 1950s. In that time, the population has dwindled from about 2 million to less than half that. Bustling neighborhoods have vanished, leaving behind lonely houses with crumbling porches and jack-o'-lantern windows. On these sprawling urban prairies, feral dogs and pheasants stalk streets with debris strewn like driftwood: an empty mail crate, a discarded winter jacket, a bunny-eared TV in tall grass. Asked recently about a dip in the city's murder rate, a mayoral candidate deadpanned, "I don't mean to be sarcastic, but there just isn't anyone left to kill."

Detroit's motto, coined in 1827 to memorialize a devastating fire, translates from Latin as "We hope for better things; it shall arise from the ashes." And if Detroit is the nexus of the Rust Belt's decay, it's also a signpost for where other ailing cities may be headed—

"To me, this is war. And I think we're going to win."

—GEORGE JACKSON, CEO, DETROIT ECONOMIC GROWTH CORPORATION

and a laboratory for the sort of radical reconstruction needed to fend off urban decline. "We're not going to roll over and die," says George Jackson, CEO of the Detroit Economic Growth Corporation. "To me, this is war. And I think we're going to win."

What would a new Detroit look like? Many say it will have to be smaller, greener and denser. The approximately one-third of the city lying empty or unused is not just an emblem of its corrosion but also the blank slate on which to chart a path to renewal. So Detroit is moving on. In place of assembly lines, hundreds of urban farms and gardens have taken root. Nonprofit organizations are helping residents transform barren neighborhoods into fertile plots that feed impoverished families, beautify blighted blocks and raise home values. Among the ideas are the reforestation of the city's dead zones; the planting of large-scale networks of parks and commercial farms; and schemes to repurpose unused space, such as in the Brightmoor neighborhood, where Justin Hollander, an urban-planning professor at Tufts University, suggests converting vacant housing into parking lots that would accommodate local trucking concerns.

For those who have already written the city's obituary, plans to shrink or green Detroit are merely cosmetic solutions to terminal decline. Detroit faces a unique tableau of challenges, from the moribund car industry to its thousands of unemployed, its tattered public-school system and the income gulf separating its slums from the McMansions of Oakland County next door. But it's hardly the first town to rust when its economic engines sputtered. As an example, experts cite Youngstown, Ohio—a dying steel city attempting to revive its fortunes by curbing population sprawl, embracing green industries and slashing residential land use 30%.

As America's 11th largest city tries to mount a comeback, locals battling lean times are far from the only stakeholders. "The problems facing Detroit are definitely going to be cropping up in cities all over the country," says Hollander. "The kind of devastated postindustrial landscape we associate with the Rust Belt is starting to creep into the Sun Belt and may start to become a universal problem." And that's why the world is now watching Detroit with interest, waiting to see if it finds a way to rise from the ashes. ——BY ALEX ALTMAN

Faded glory *Fisher Body #21, an auto body assembly plant, was built*

in 1919 by brothers Fred and Charles Fisher; it closed in the early 1990s. Local artist Scott Hocking created the pyramid, a commentary on decline

Canary, swallowed
From left, Williams, Stone and Dorsey are the latest update of a now familiar archetype: software visionaries who are reshaping our world

Evan Williams, Biz Stone, Jack Dorsey

Together, they're known as "the Twitter guys." And they've set the Internet aflutter

WHEN JACK DORSEY, EVAN WILLIAMS AND BIZ STONE founded Twitter in 2006, they were probably worried about things like making money and protecting people's privacy and drunk college kids breaking up with one another in "tweets," brief Internet text messages of 140 characters or less. What they weren't worried about was being suppressed by the Iranian government. But in the networked, surreally flattened world of Internet social media, those things aren't as far apart as they used to be—and in 2009 what began as a toy for online flirtation suddenly was being put to much more serious uses. After the election in Iran, most cries of protest from supporters of opposition candidate Mir-Hossein

Mousavi were shut down by authorities, but those that got through appeared on a medium that didn't even exist the last time Iran had an election.

So what makes Twitter the medium of the moment? It's free, highly mobile, very personal and very quick. It's also built to spread, and fast. Twitterers like to append notes called hashtags—#theylooklikethis—to their tweets, so that they can be grouped and searched for by topic; especially interesting or urgent tweets tend to get picked up and retransmitted by other Twitterers, a practice known as retweeting, or just RT. Tweets go out over two networks, the Internet and SMS, the network that cell phones use for text messages, and they can be received and read on practically anything with a screen and a network connection. The resulting rapid-fire network has taken real-time Internet communication into a new age that industry pioneer John Batelle calls "the super-fresh Web."

Williams, 37, Stone, 35, and Dorsey, 33, are a central-casting vision of Internet start-up savvy. They're quotable and charming and have the extra glamour of using a loft in San Francisco's SoMa district as a headquarters instead of a bland office park in Silicon Valley. Software guru Dorsey created Twitter in 2006, when he was employed at a now defunct podcasting company called Odeo, which was run by entrepreneur Williams. Dorsey, Williams, and Stone, another Odeo software savant, spun out Twitter in August 2007, with Dorsey at the helm; he is now chairman of the board, while Williams is CEO and Stone is Creative Director. Within two years, Twitter was moving the earth. Mind you, it isn't making money yet. But we wouldn't bet against the Twitter guys.

Bernard Madoff

For too long, investors paid no attention to the man behind the golden curtain—until he turned out to be running a scam

FOR YEARS, BERNIE MADOFF WAS REGARDED AS A pillar of New York City's investment community, a taciturn superstar with a sterling reputation whose clockwork, ever expanding returns had would-be clients nearly breaking down his door on the 17th floor of the Lipstick Building in Manhattan. But late in 2008, the world learned that the 70-year-old money manager had been presiding over a fraudulent criminal empire, bilking thousands of investors, picking the deep pockets of his country-club counterparts, bankrupting charitable foundations and ransacking tycoons and celebrities alike. His trademark thin-lipped smile became the defining image of the avarice that in the fall of 2008 nearly brought the global financial system to its knees.

One hesitates to bestow superlatives upon a crook, but Madoff's long-running Ponzi scheme, which came to a screeching halt with his Dec. 11,

2008, arrest, is very likely history's biggest financial swindle, estimated by authorities to total $64.8 billion. On March 12, 2009, Madoff entered a guilty plea to all 11 federal offenses with which he was charged, including securities fraud, wire fraud, mail fraud, money laundering, perjury and making false filings with the SEC. No plea bargain was involved. Before he was sentenced to serve 150 years in prison, Madoff addressed his investors in the courtroom and offered an apology: "I have left a legacy of shame, as some of my victims have pointed out, to my family and my grandchildren. This is something I will live in for the rest of my life. I'm sorry." And then he added words that chilled: "I know that doesn't help you."

After the sentencing, Federal Judge Denny Chin ordered Madoff remanded to New York City's Metropolitan Correctional Center—a bit of a step down from his $9.9 million Upper East Side apartment.

Perp walk *Paparazzi train their lenses on Madoff in New York City on March 12, the day he pleaded guilty to all charges*

In Brief

ESSENTIAL STORIES / SOCIETY & BUSINESS

Technology
Comeback of The Year, No. 1

Few executives are more closely identified with their company's success than Apple's Steve Jobs, 54. But in recent years Jobs has battled pancreatic cancer and other ailments that have left him looking gaunt and fatigued. In January Apple announced that Jobs would be taking a health leave of absence for six months—and then clammed up.

So Apple fans cheered on Sept. 9, when Jobs, left, strode onstage at an annual Apple conference and said surgery to replace his liver, affected by the cancer, had been a success.

Also a success: Apple's iPhone. Jobs said Apple had sold 30 million of the devices in two years, and that 1.8 billion applications had been downloaded for them.

Religion

AN UNEXPECTED INVITATION *Pope Benedict XVI surprised members of two flocks in October when he announced the Roman Catholic Church would create a new structure to welcome some disenchanted Anglicans into its fold. Under the new "Personal Ordinariates," Anglicans, including married priests, can practice Catholicism while preserving much of their own identity and liturgy. Anglican leaders are struggling to avoid a full-fledged schism as battles over women and gay clergy have plagued their 80-million-strong church, which includes 2.2 million American Episcopalians. Archbishop of Canterbury Rowan Williams said that the Pope's offer "brings an end to a period of uncertainty" for those Anglicans who have sought to convert. But some Anglicans were offended by the Pope's offer, branding it an attempt to poach for converts from among their faithful.*

Publishing
Stop the Presses—Forever

Battered by two crushing forces—an economic downturn that sent advertising revenues plunging in all media, and the ongoing migration of readers from print to digital formats—a number of the nation's most familiar newspapers printed their final issues in 2009. Among them: the Seattle *Post-Intelligencer* and Denver's *Rocky Mountain News.* In the magazine world, Condé Nast shuttered its venerable *Gourmet* title after almost 70 years of publication.

Crime
Killing in the Cause of Life

Wichita, Kans., physician George Tiller, 67, was one of only three U.S. doctors who performed late-term abortions; in 1993 he was shot and wounded by a pro-life activist. Tiller recovered, but he remained the target of protests. On May 31, he was shot and killed; pro-life advocate Scott Roeder, 51, was charged with the crime.

Technology
Twitter's Next Frontier

Online, 2009 was the Year of Twitter: the fast-paced social network became the application of the hour, much like Amazon, Google, YouTube and Facebook before it. As with YouTube, Twitter execs are still wrestling with a basic Internet paradox: it's one thing to attract tens of millions of dedicated users—and quite another to convert their eyeballs into hard dollars. One attempt: in 2009 online marketer Izea launched a program called "Sponsored Tweets." As of October, 700 advertisers had signed on. Spam, ahoy!

Business
Power Failures

As the shock waves from the U.S. economic meltdown in 2008 rippled through the economy in 2009, a number of major retailers were forced to shut down operations, while many others closed ailing branches, trimmed employee rolls and cut costs wherever possible. Among the most troubled retailers:

Circuit City The No. 2 consumer electronics chain in the U.S. filed for bankruptcy early

in November 2008 and shut down all its stores in March.

Linens 'n Things The big household chain shut down most of its operations in the last week of 2008 and announced in 2009 it would maintain an online presence with a severely downsized business model.

Among other chains on the ropes Talbots, Pier 1 Imports, Office Depot, Borders books.

Food
Comeback of the Year, No. 2

Don't it always seem to go, that you don't know what you've got till it's gone? Thanks to the hit film *Julie & Julia*, which portrayed the popular TV chef Julia Child, above, who died in 2004, as an aspiring Cordon Bleu student in Paris in the 1950s, Americans again took up Child-ish things, and her chef d'oeuvre, *Mastering the Art of French Cooking*, topped best-seller lists for the first time.

Society
Gay Marriage: The Great Divide

Yolonda Johnson-Foster, left, and Amy Foster tear up as they are married in Iowa City on May 1, 2009. Gay marriage was legalized in Iowa in April 2009; it is illegal in Missouri, where the pair reside. As of November 2009, gay marriage was legal in six states and had been outlawed by popular vote in 31 others. Legalization was narrowly voted down by Maine voters on Nov. 3.

Victory Laps. Roger, Serena and Kobe do it again—but a fresh crop of stars is rocking the sports world

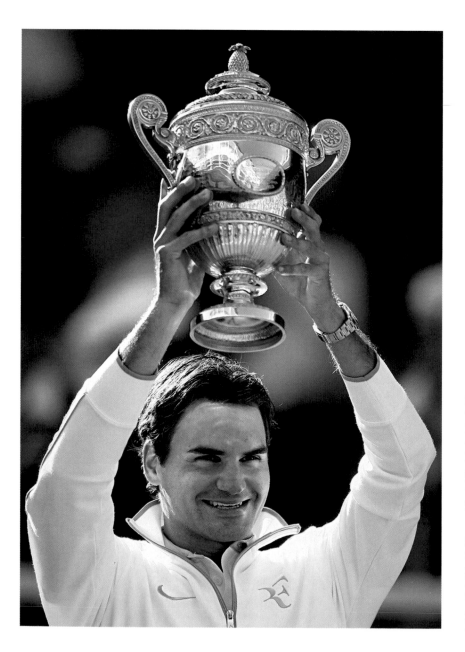

Roger Reigns Alone

The great Swiss player Roger Federer lost the Australian Open to his longtime rival, the Spaniard Rafael Nadal. But with Nadal later injured, Federer snagged his first French Open crown, then beat American Andy Roddick at Wimbledon, left, to win his 15th major title, breaking Pete Sampras' record. Federer, 28, is now widely called the greatest player in tennis history, despite his surprising loss in the U.S. Open finals in September to Argentina's strong young star, Juan Martin del Potro.

The Lakers: Untouchable

Kobe Bryant (No. 24) and the Los Angeles Lakers cruised to a commanding 4-1 victory over the outmatched Orlando Magic in the 2009 NBA finals. Bryant, 31, iced his status as a go-to franchise player, and the title gave L.A. coach Phil Jackson his 10th NBA championship, surpassing the nine won by legendary Boston Celtics coach Red Auerbach.

No Country for Old Men

Tom Watson, far right, is a beloved elder in the golf world. At Britain's Open Championship at Turnberry in July, the five-time Open champ, then 59, thrilled fans by holding onto a lead going into the last round. But Watson faded, bogeying the 72nd hole, and American Stewart Cink, 36, left—a popular favorite, if not yet a legend—took home the Claret Jug in a playoff.

La Serenissima—Not!

Women's tennis may seem stuck in a rut, as the Sisters Williams—Serena, 28, left, and sibling Venus, 29—squared off for the eighth time in the final match of a Grand Slam tourney at Wimbledon. Yet the rivalry remains compelling. Serena won, nabbing her third silver platter at Centre Court. But in the U.S. Open final, Serena threw a hissy fit at a line judge as she lost to Belgian Kim Clijsters.

U.S. Soccer Heads Up

Know hope, U.S. soccer fans: that's America's Oguchi Onyewu going up for the ball against Brazil at left, as the U.S. national team played in the finals of a major international tournament for the first time. Brazil won, 3-2, to take the Confederations Cup title in South Africa, but the Americans proved they've got game—and in October they beat Honduras, 3-2, to earn a chance to play in the 2010 World Cup.

A Run for the History Books

The Kentucky Derby may have seen more exciting races than the 2009 event, but even the oldest railbirds couldn't recall when. At top right, Calvin Borel, the 2007 winning rider, crosses the finish line on Mine That Bird, after bringing the 50-to-1 underdog all the way from the back of the pack to win by almost seven lengths. It was the Derby's longest margin of victory in more than 60 years.

A New Pair of Aces

Watching the Rogers and Tigers of sports rewrite the record books is great fun. But we need new stars too—and 2009 provided them, in the form of South Korea's Yang Yong-eun, 37, near right, who beat a collapsing Tiger Woods in the PGA Championship; and in Argentina's Juan Martin del Potro, 21. Serving rockets, the 6-ft. 6-in. Del Potro, far right, whipped Roger Federer in the U.S. Open.

TOP: CLIVE BURNSKILL—GETTY IMAGES; BOTTOM: JEFF MITCHELL—FIFA VIA GETTY IMAGES

The Steelers Return to Glory

In an NFL year that will be recalled for serving up a host of dramatic finishes, the Pittsburgh Steelers under quarterback Ben Roethlisberger scored a thrilling win over a tough Arizona Cardinals squad in Super Bowl XLIII. After Arizona took the lead with 2:37 remaining in the game, Santonio Holmes, above, hauled in a 6-yd. toss with only 35 seconds left on the clock to bring the Steelers their sixth Super Bowl victory, an NFL record.

The Yanks (and A-Rod) Come Back

The baseball playoffs offered spine-tingling contests in both leagues, but the biggest story was the hitting of New York Yankees third baseman Alex Rodriguez, 34, left. The slugger had compiled a dismal record in post-season play in previous years, but this time around he batted .438, hit 5 home runs and notched 12 runs batted to lead the Yankees to the World Series against the talented, power-hitting Philadelphia Phillies, the reigning world champs. The Yanks, with veterans Derek Jeter, Mariano Rivera and Andy Pettitte in fine form, won their 27th world championship and first since 2000 in six games.

OPPOSITE: HORACIO VILLALOBOS—EPA—CORBIS. THIS PAGE, TOP: G. NEWMAN LOWRANCE—GETTY IMAGES; BOTTOM: JAE C. HONG—AP IMAGES

Eyes on the Prize

Lance Armstrong had already made one comeback for the ages: diagnosed with testicular cancer in 1996, he was given less than a 50% chance of survival. Not only did he make it through, but he got back on his bike, picked up his cycling career and proceeded to win seven Tour de France titles in a row, from 1999 to 2005. Now, four years later, he decided to tour France again. In Europe, allegations of drug use have dogged the American in the past, and he was out to prove he didn't need drugs to win. But what Armstrong did need was the support of his Astana teammates, and they were badly riven, forced to choose between the veteran Armstrong, then 37, and a young rival, Spanish star Alberto Contador, left, 26.

An ugly duel emerged, and matters got uglier after Contador went ahead of Armstrong in the Alps and went on to win the race; Armstrong finished third. "He is a great rider and has completed a great race, but ... I have never had great admiration for him and I never will," Contador said of his foe. The American replied: "If I were him, I'd drop this drivel and start thanking his team. Without them, he doesn't win."

In Brief

ESSENTIAL STORIES

Football

WIDE-OPEN SPACES *The team is the Cowboys, the home state is Texas, and the owner is the NFL's flashiest showman, Jerry Jones—small wonder his new Cowboys Stadium is an exercise in excess. The Cowboys played their first game in the $1.2 billion pleasure dome on Sept. 20, with a big show for 105,121 fans. Highlights: 325 luxury suites; a retractable roof; a mammoth, four-sided Cleopatra's barge of video screens stretching 160 ft. in length; and George W. Bush tossing the coin. The cheapest "seats" in the house are $29 each, for standing room above the end zones.*

Olympics

No Rings for Chicago

Major world cities are now spending years—and tens of millions of dollars—to be chosen to play host to the Olympic Games by the voters of the International Olympic Committee. As the decision for the 2016 Summer Games drew near, President Obama flew to Copenhagen to twist arms for Chicago's bid—but it was the *cariocas* of Rio de Janeiro in Brazil who ended up rejoicing: theirs will be South America's first city to host the games.

Auto Racing

Chasing Glory

Never play cards with a man called Doc. Never eat at a place called Mom's. And on the NASCAR circuit, they're adding a new entry to Nelson Algren's to-don't list: don't go racing stock cars against a guy named Jimmie. Racing fans' eyes were on veteran Jimmie Johnson, 34, as the California native was gunning to break out of his tie with the legendary Cale

Yarborough: they are the only two drivers to have won the season-ending championship, now called the Sprint Cup, three times. As of mid-October, Johnson was first in the Cup standings.

Golf
It's Official—They're Human

Phil Mickelson and Tiger Woods were all smiles on Sept. 27, above. Mickelson, 39, had just beaten Woods in the Tour Championship tourney in Atlanta, while Woods, 33, took home the FedEx Cup, the PGA's new end-of-season multievent challenge, making him $10 million richer. But in fact, Mickelson's year was tough, as both his wife and mother battled breast cancer, while Woods failed to win a major title in 2009, losing the PGA Championship after entering the final round with a four-stroke lead.

Basketball
Err Jordan

It was a night for grand memories, as the NBA welcomed, from left, Vivian Stringer, Michael Jordan, John Stockton, David Robinson and Jerry Sloan to its Hall of Fame. But Jordan threw an airball, using his speech to settle old scores and dig up old grudges—leaving fans and commentators alike crying foul.

Football
Brett's Riposte

There is no sadder sight in sports than an aging icon who doesn't know when to hang up his uniform. For a while there, it seemed as if the Green Bay Packers' legendary quarterback Brett Favre was on that path. He retired after the 2007 season, then changed his mind—but the Pack sent him packing anyway.

Favre, below, played for the New York Jets in 2008, starting strong but ending up with a gimpy right wing. But in 2009 the magic was back, early on at least, as Favre, who turned 40 in October, and his new team, the Minnesota Vikings, beat San Francisco's 49ers with two seconds left, then whipped the Pack, 30-23. Revenge!

Comeback *After Michael Vick, 29, served 21 months in prison for his 2007 conviction for abusing animals in a dog-fighting ring, the star quarterback joined the Philadelphia Eagles*

Crime Blotter

Yes, we also wish that there were no need for a list of off-field bad deeds on the sports pages, but as athletes and coaches continue to act up, society is no longer looking away.

STEVE MCNAIR
The popular onetime Tennessee Titans quarterback died of gunshot wounds on July 4, at 36. His alleged mistress, Sahel Kazemi, 20, who was found dead at his side, killed him in a murder-suicide, Nashville prosecutors said.

PLAXICO BURRESS
The New York Giants wide receiver, 32, was sentenced to two years in jail after pleading guilty to illegal possession of a firearm, following a November 2008 incident in which he shot himself in the leg when a pistol he was carrying went off in a New York City nightclub.

RICK PITINO
The veteran basketball coach, 57, who runs the successful program at the University of Louisville, told police he had been the victim of an extortion plot devised by a onetime mistress, Karen Sypher. She was indicted by a grand jury; he apologized and university authorities said he would remain in his post.

Arts

◻ Arts groups struggled amid the economic downturn, yet even so, Dallas, Chicago and New York City were among American cities opening new museum buildings and performing arts spaces in 2009. In tough times, audiences seemed content to gaze in the rear-view mirror, as sequels lit up movie screens, the Beatles found new worlds to conquer, Scotland gave the world an old-school singing sensation, and Britney Spears enjoyed a comeback tour—at age 27.

LYLE A. WAISMAN—GETTY IMAGES

Top this! *U2, widely considered the world's foremo*

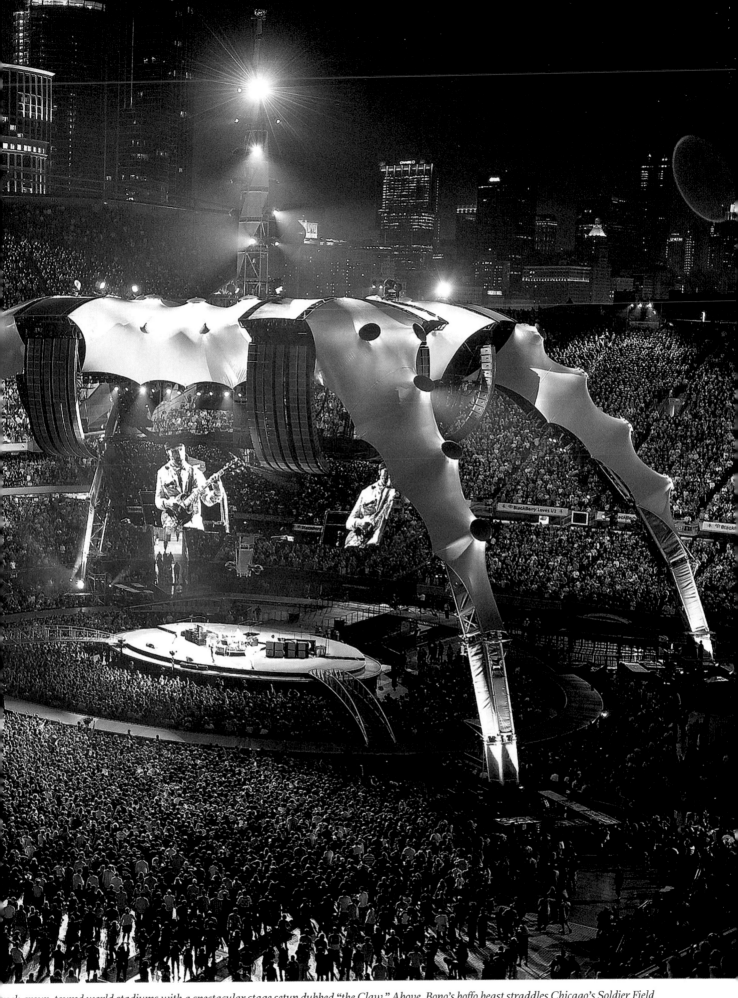

rock group, toured world stadiums with a spectacular stage setup dubbed "the Claw." Above, Bono's boffo beast straddles Chicago's Soldier Field

Free rein *Kandinsky's horsemen in* Blue Mountain *(1908-09), left, held a symbolic meaning as emblems of expressive freedom. Influenced by the crackling Fauvist pictures of Henri Matisse and André Derain, the artist was galloping full speed in the direction of complete abstraction*

The Worlds Within

Expressing spiritual longings in abstract form, Wassily Kandinsky and Georgia O'Keeffe aimed to achieve escape velocity on canvas

IT'S BEEN A LONG TIME SINCE ABSTRACT ART WAS A religion. For most artists now, it's just an option, a mode they can pursue or ignore as it suits them. But once it was a passion, a polemic, a faith. Wassily Kandinsky, one of its founders, could talk about geometric forms as though they were sacred images—and to him, they were. In a burst of high feeling he could argue, with a straight face, that "the contact between the acute angle of a triangle and a circle has no less effect than that of God's finger touching Adam's in Michelangelo." They just don't make triangles like that anymore.

By a happy coincidence of programming, two of New York City's biggest museums looked back in the fall of 2009 on those exalted beginnings. "Kandinsky," at the Solomon R. Guggenheim Museum, sent nearly 100 of the artist's works up the Guggenheim's spiral ramp like

a whirlpool of angels in a Tiepolo ceiling. Meanwhile, at the Whitney Museum of American Art, "Georgia O'Keeffe: Abstraction" scraped away O'Keeffe's barnacled legend as the Gray Lady of New Mexico to recall the young woman who at the dawn of abstraction made a fearless leap into the unknown.

Born in 1866 to a prosperous Moscow family, Kandinsky, who would become the most tireless apostle of an art that answered to nothing in the merely material world, spent his 20s studying law and economics, all the while bending toward another calling. In 1896, with his first wife Anja, he decamped to Munich to become an artist and art teacher. His early paintings were folkloric, storybook scenes of an imaginary medieval Russia. It wasn't until the summer of 1908, when he discovered the little town of Murnau in the Bavarian Alps, that he

Unfolding *In her early abstract works, including Series 1, No. 4 (1918), O'Keeffe drew from nature, Art Nouveau and her interior life. Her first such works were created in charcoal, but she soon moved on to painting rich colors in oil*

began to uncouple his pictures from any source in the visible world. In *Blue Mountain* (1908-09), he assigned the mountain an unearthly shade of indigo and turned the flanking trees into almost free-floating pools of pigment. He was on the way to letting form and color alone become the subject of his work. For him, abstract images were also representations of a kind, correlatives of spiritual realities. He was an admirer of the Russian mystic Madame Blavatsky, founder of Theosophy, a stew of beliefs about a spiritual realm superior to the material world, and he saw his work as a search for forms and colors that would speak the language of that higher plane.

O'Keeffe, who owned a copy of Kandinsky's book *Concerning the Spiritual in Art,* was no Theosophist, but like him, she felt that abstract art could express internal realities. In 1915 she was a 28-year-old art teacher stuck at a small women's college in South Carolina, one year removed from art studies in New York City, where she had got her first eager taste of Picasso, Braque and American modernists like John Marin. Stranded in a place she called the "tail end of the world," she decided to go where none of those artists had ventured. Drawing on

the liquid forms of Art Nouveau and her own churning inner life, she produced an astonishing series of purely abstract charcoal drawings, some of the most radical work being done anywhere at that moment.

Within two years, during which the photographer Alfred Stieglitz, her future husband, gave her a solo exhibition in New York that made her name for good, O'Keeffe had reintroduced color into her work. Her typical canvases were eruptions of soft form, like the cresting fiddleheads of mauve, orange and green in *Series I, No. 4*, from 1918. But she also worked in a taut, sharp-edged register. And if the plump bulbs of color and shadowy openings of some of these works evoke the swells and inlets of the female body, the Whitney show refreshingly spared us the caricature of O'Keeffe as Earth Mother and pointed us back to the endlessly inventive formalist she remained, intermittently, to the end of her life.

Abstraction may not be a religion anymore, but you can't look at the early buoyant pictures in either of these shows without being glad that, for a while, there were artists who kept the faith.

—*By Richard Lacayo*

113

Screen Gems. Our critics eye the year's best—and worst—films

MAYBE *SUNSET BOULEVARD* GOT IT WRONG: THE TROUBLE WITH today's pictures isn't that they got small—the trouble is, they got too big. The year's biggest box-office hit was the special-effects epic *Transformers 2: Revenge of the Fallen.* TIME's critics hated it. On these pages, Mary Pols and Richard Corliss weigh in, no holds barred, on some of the movies that transformed audiences rather than robots.

THE YEAR IN MOVIES

District 9

District 9 is a grimy little scare-fi thriller from South Africa, hitherto unknown as a production center for really cool movies. Its real star is director and co-writer Neill Blomkamp, 29, who proves with his first feature that no genre is so tarnished by overuse and misuse that it can't be revived by a smart kid with fresh ideas.

Blomkamp pours his clever notions into a familiar mold: a story of extraterrestrials who come to Earth and are treated like out-laws. Evicted and imprisoned, deprived of their rights, the aliens could be the Palestinians in Gaza, the detainees in Guantánamo or black South Africans for the 46 years of apartheid and, in effect, for centuries before. This feature-film novice director sells his vision of Johannesburg as a dusty sump hole, a place of sapping heat and blinding glare.

—RICHARD CORLISS

Up

It started with a cartoon drawing: a cluster of gaily colored party balloons held by a cranky old man, his eyes asquint, as if daring any kid to take one. Pete Docter's sketch, made back in '04, suggested another droll innovation at Pixar, a studio proud of taking risks in a traditional genre; *mean* and *old* are words rarely attached to the main character in an animated feature. But Docter, 41, and his co-director and co-writer Bob Peterson didn't want just to have fun with the elderly gent. They would send him and the audience on a journey in two new directions: penetratingly inward and exaltedly up. *Up* is the studio's most deeply emotional and affecting work.

—RC

Julie & Julia

Director Nora Ephron's movie is based on the book of the same name, Julie Powell's account of the year she spent cooking her way through Julia Child's *Mastering the Art of French Cooking* and blogging about her experiences. *Julie & Julia* is structured around the idea of two women "finding" themselves, but in its examination of the way talent, hard work and ambition are doled out in unequal measures to different women—both ultimately successful—it's got an undercurrent of *All About Eve*. Meryl Streep's Child is better than a basket of kittens. The performance is a hoot and a joy. This is a charming crowd pleaser, but it's also surprisingly bold. Ephron has varied her usual moviemaking recipe, proof that Julia Child still inspires.

—MARY POLS

Food, Inc.

Robert Kenner's passionate, witty documentary traces our evolution from an agrarian nation to one of monoculture—approximately 30% of U.S. cropland is planted with corn. We meet the meat, most of it miserable, corn-fed, dosed with antibiotics and on its way to centralized slaughterhouses and processing plants. Kenner shows us farmers in peril, powerful corporations in charge, scientists cooking up genetically modified foods and the toll the system takes on our health and sometimes even our lives. —MP

THUMBS DOWN

Transformers 2: Revenge of the Fallen

Revenge is director Michael Bay at his purest: gleaming machines, humans that glisten with an omnipresent layer of sweat, dozens of locations and a story line so messy it borders on the abstract. He's even given one of the robot Decepticons testicles (brass, swinging). The whole experience is like having your nose pressed into Bay's manly armpit for well over 2 hours. —MP

BEST ACTRESS

Kate Winslet

She can do almost anything, be almost anyone, as long as the code word is danger. A ticket to a Kate Winslet movie pays for a trip into uncharted lands and toxic emotions. She doesn't play weak; she's not in it for the fun. She looks over the edge, leaps in and takes you down with her. This English actress, 34, has been a force for sizzle and discomfort since she was a teenager, in Peter Jackson's *Heavenly Creatures*, in which she propelled another girl onto a murderous fantasy ride. In *Titanic*, her biggest hit and least jangling role, she was the aristocratic love and death of poor boy Leonardo DiCaprio. *Jude, Iris, Eternal Sunshine of the Spotless Mind*: they all cast her as the dominant female force. That suited Winslet, since her intelligence as an actress is essentially critical; it gives an erotic taunt and charge to any encounter. Winslet women usually proceed from an enveloping restlessness, a resentment of the status quo. This life isn't enough; let's stir things up.

In *The Reader* (for which she received the Oscar award as Best Actress in 2009), Winslet puts across all of Hanna Schmitz's misery, moral blind spots and allure in a performance of precise and desperate passion. Come fly with me, her laser stare says—to hell. —RC

115

Urban Uplift

The imaginative makeover of an abandoned train line turns a Manhattan eyesore into 21st century eye candy

CITY PLANNERS CALL IT "ADAPTIVE REUSE." We call it magic. Capping a 10-year effort, on June 9 New York City opened the High Line Park, an innovative slice of nature created on elevated train tracks built in the 1930s that had been deteriorating for decades. The ribbon of green winds above gritty city streets for some 1.45 miles (2.33 km) along Manhattan's Lower West Side, close by the Hudson River. A second section that will extend the park north for another 10 blocks is under construction. The heroes of the rebirth are neighborhood residents Robert Hammond and Joshua David, who first proposed the park, and architectural firm Diller Scofidio + Renfro, which designed it, with a nod to a similarly reimagined railway viaduct in Paris, the snazzy Promenade Plantée, which opened in 1998.

New Yorkers and visitors to the city have eagerly embraced the park, which offers unexpected views of both the Hudson River and the Chelsea neighborhood, which has become the center of the city's visual arts scene in the past 15 years. One local resident began offering cabaret performances on her fire escape, and New York City Mayor Michael Bloomberg said the imaginative new space had sparked the creation of some 30 new building projects near its path. Similar skyways are now being considered by Chicago, Philadelphia and several other U.S. cities.

ANDY KROPA—REDUXT

Above it all *The High Line's architects chose to plant native species of grasses and*

flowers along the path and kept numerous reminders of its original use as an elevated train line, including stretches of train tracks and ties

Now Appearing. Britney rocks out live, the Beatles go virtual and Broadway thanks its lucky stars

THE YEAR IN MUSIC

Fab Faux
The Beatles took over both the pop charts and the videogame world on 9/9/09. Ringo Starr, 69, and Paul McCartney, 67 (shown above at the game's industry-expo kick-off), worked with designers to put the Apple imprimatur on the new Beatles Rock Band game, which lets fans sing and play along to the group's peerless songlist. The 13 original Beatles albums were released in newly remastered form on the same day. TIME's verdict, 45 years on: "They all sound great."

Younger Hands on the Baton
Two of America's most admired symphony orchestras welcomed dynamic new conductors to their podiums in 2009. Alan Gilbert, 42 (above), took over from Lorin Maazel at the New York Philharmonic; he is the son of two longtime Philharmonic violinists. The Los Angeles Philharmonic will now be led by the brilliant Venezuelan conductor and violinist Gustavo Dudamel, left, who is only 28. Bravo!

On the Road Again

Britney Spears and the Jonas Brothers, below, were among those mounting major tours in a year when fans' ticket funds were scanty.

JONAS BROTHERS *World Tour*
Still on top as the galaxy's most popular boy band, the bros (from left, Joe, Kevin and Nick) launched a world tour

U2 *The 360° Tour*
Bono & Co. toured the world, Claw in tow, supporting a new album, *No Line on the Horizon*

BRITNEY SPEARS *The Circus Tour*
Newly svelte and newly sensible, Spears, now 27, sold out arenas in North America, Europe and Australia

Back to the Future for '80s Rockers

Rock of Ages, the latest in Broadway's parade—or plague, as some call it—of jukebox musicals, toasted the sounds of the 1980s, featuring arena anthems by such titans of yesteryear as Styx and Whitesnake. The New York *Times* hailed it as "seriously silly and absurdly enjoyable," but TIME's Richard Zoglin found it "witless" and scolded Tony judges for its Best Musical nomination.

Seductive Starlight

Broadway audiences just won't stomach straight plays without a side order of stardust, it seems. In 2009 Hugh Jackman, Daniel Craig and James Gandolfini lit up Broadway marquees and ignited ticket sales. At left, Bill Irwin, John Goodman and Nathan Lane won raves in Samuel Beckett's classic *Waiting for Godot*.

Broadway Bows to the Rule of Law

Britain's Jude Law first appeared on Broadway in 1995, when he was 22, with Kathleen Turner, Roger Rees and Cynthia Nixon in a production of the 1938 Jean Cocteau play *Les Parents Terribles* under the title *Indiscretions*. Fourteen years later, Law is a major star in Hollywood (*Cold Mountain*) and onstage in Britain, where his May 2009 debut as Hamlet received glowing reviews; he later played the role at Kronberg Castle in Elsinore, Denmark, the prince's home. In October Law began a limited run of the play on Broadway: TIME found him "eloquent and animated."

Buzzed *The top U.S. General in Iraq, Ray Odierno, complies with the Commander in Chief's order*

Stephen Colbert

Atten-shun! TV's two-faced man takes his show on the road

THE BEAUTY AND APPEAL OF STEPHEN COLBERT ARE that he assumes his TV alter ego—the bloviating pundit Stephen Colbert—so completely that he almost becomes whomever you want him to be. Most see his Comedy Central show, *The Colbert Report,* as a scathing satire of shrill conservative commentators like Bill O'Reilly. But some conservatives buy into the character so much that they watch it and think he's serious.

The real Stephen Colbert is 45 and, like his alter ego, was born in South Carolina as the last of 11 children. He claims to be less political—conser-

vative or otherwise—than his on-air persona. He seldom does interviews independent from his character, opting to keep his real life and political leanings more private. However, his fans wondered if there was a serious subtext to Colbert's tongue-in-cheek presidential campaign in 2007-8, which fizzled after Democratic leaders in South Carolina ruled out his bid to run in the state's primary.

Whatever his politics, the real Colbert is a strong supporter of America's men and women in uniform; he has raised tens of thousands of dollars for the United Service Organizations (USO) and other military support groups. In 2009 Colbert fused his concern for U.S. troops with his on-air persona: he teamed up with the USO to take *The Colbert Report* to Baghdad to deliver a week's worth of shows to soldiers in Iraq, a location many Americans seem to prefer to forget.

Result: a riveting series of programs that, in the words of TIME TV critic James Poniewozik, "reminded us why what Comedy Central puts on the air every night is miles more relevant than what any broadcast network is doing." On the first of his shows from Baghdad, Colbert got a closetful of shoes thrown at him, donned a crisp desert-camo suit and interviewed top General Ray Odierno, who received a hilarious satellite message from President Barack Obama: "As Commander in Chief, I hereby order you to shave that man's head!" The general obeyed, and it was a bald Colbert who went on to score a huge ratings boost with his sojourn in Iraq. Soldiers cheered when he stated, "By the power invested in me by basic cable, I officially declare that we have won the Iraq war!" Two words, Private Colbert: Mission accomplished.

Susan Boyle

She warbled, Britons marveled, YouTube beckoned—and
the world swooned. Welcome to fame, 2009-style

THE STORY OF SUSAN BOYLE IS, EXCEPT TO THE most
jaded and curmudgeonly among us, completely
irresistible. Fished, seemingly, from the bottom of
the troll pond by *Britain's Got Talent,* this humble,
working-class, physically ill-favored soul was
suddenly found to be capable of creating music
of astonishing beauty. People reacted as if vast
quantities of treasure had been discovered in the
trunk of a broken-down Hyundai abandoned on
their street—it was always there, but nobody had
ever bothered to look. Thanks to the grouchy Simon
Cowell (and YouTube), Boyle soon became an overnight sensation, as millions worldwide joined the
show's judges in discovering lumps in their throats
and tears in their eyes.

Ugly-duckling stories don't get any better than
this. And *Britain's Got Talent* milked it for all it was
worth, cutting away to eye rolls and snickering by
the audience and judges before Boyle's wow-induc-
ing rendition of the *Les Miz* warhorse *I Dreamed
a Dream.* (Eye rolls and snickering, of course, can
be taped at any time and edited in later, but never
mind.) Boyle's backstory: now 48, she was one of
nine children whose father worked in a car factory
and mother in a typing pool. She was unemployed
and, yes, living alone with her cat, Pebbles, in Black-
burn, Scotland. She had taken singing lessons and
recorded *Cry Me a River* for a charity CD in 1999. An
observant Catholic, she often sang at church and on
karaoke nights. What held Boyle back was caring
for her aging parents. She entered *BGT,* after her
mother died, because she was approached by talent
scouts from the show—this Cinderella had a date
to the ball.

Then came the stunning dénouement to this
unlikely tale: in the show's finale, Boyle was upset
by Diversity, a hip-hop dance troupe. Afterward,
she was admitted to a London clinic, for "exhaustion." What happened? Some argued that Boyle had
become too much of a foregone conclusion, possibly
sparking a backlash. And there were press reports
of a public temper tantrum. The show's producers
were blamed for plucking Boyle from obscurity and

Songbird *Boyle was "Scotland's least processed export since
steel-cut porridge oats," observed* TIME's *Catherine Mayer*

subjecting her to the pressure of overnight fame—
often by the same people who a few weeks earlier
were saying how wonderful it was that the show
had plucked her from obscurity and rewarded her
with overnight fame. Alas for Susan: as David Bowie
tried to warn her: "Fame/Puts you there where
things are hollow."

In Brief

ESSENTIAL STORIES

Architecture

LINCOLN CENTER'S NEW LOOK *Built in the 1960s, New York City's Lincoln Center was shiny and aloof from the streets around it. Now the arts complex is getting a $1.2 billion makeover, kicking off with chamber-music auditorium Alice Tully Hall, re-imagined by Diller, Scofidio + Renfro. Said* TIME *critic Richard Lacayo: "To open up the building, [the architects] more or less exploded it. At one triangular corner they greatly extended the lobby, wrapped it in glass and stacked a glass-walled dance-rehearsal space just above. That transparent box cantilevers over the street to offer free performances for whoever walks by—like a JumboTron but with real people dancing inside it."*

Television

Late Night's Wake-Up Call

After years of stasis, late-night TV got all shook up in 2009—and that was before David Letterman spilled the beans. Jay Leno moved to prime time, Conan O'Brien took over Jay's old spot, and Jimmy Fallon entered the lists.

CONAN O'BRIEN
The cerebral comic may be an acquired taste; his *Late Night* show on NBC took years to catch on. He's hoping history repeats itself: in the first months after he began hosting the *Tonight Show* in June, ratings took a steep dive.

JAY LENO
In one of the biggest gambles in TV history, longtime *Tonight Show* host Jay Leno is helming a new NBC variety show that will run five nights a week in the prime 10 to 11 p.m. (E.S.T.) time period. The show will be far cheaper to mount than a scripted series, say NBC execs.

JIMMY FALLON
The popular *Saturday Night Live* funnyman took over from Conan O'Brien as host of NBC's *Late Show* in March. It's still early, but the show is performing well against CBS's *The Late Late Show with Craig Ferguson.*

Books

Symbols Lost, Dollars Found

He's back! Or, rather, *they're* back: ace symbologist Robert Langdon and his creator, best-seller-list Bigfoot Dan Brown, turned Sept. 15 into Christmas for booksellers, when Brown's *The Lost Symbol* was published in a huge first printing of 5 million copies.

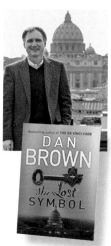

Brown's fans, who bought some 80 million copies of his 2003 breakthrough, *The Da Vinci Code*, quickly sent the new tale of Masonic symbols in U.S. national monuments to the top of the lists. TIME critic Lev Grossman's comment: "It's fun, but you feel a little bruised afterward."

Painting
Visions of Vermeer

Q. How many paintings does it take to mount a major show? *A.* One, when the museum involved is New York City's Metropolitan Museum of Art, the painter is Jan Vermeer, and the work, on loan from Amsterdam's famed Rijksmuseum, is *The Milkmaid,* an exquisite portrait dated to circa 1658. The Met rounded out the smash exhibit with five of its own Vermeers.

Opera
Tosca? Basta!

When former recording executive Peter Gelb became general manager of New York City's Metropolitan Opera in 2006, he vowed to update its aging, if beloved, productions. But on opening night of the 2009 season, Met audiences loudly booed Swiss director Luc Bondy's stark, dark new staging of Puccini's *Tosca.*

Pop Culture
A Phalanx Of Phangs

Say *aaaahhh* … and scowl. Vampires maintained their grip on pop culture in 2009, a trend that began with the success of Stephenie Meyer's *Twilight* series of fantasy/romance novels. The first film adaptation of Meyer's sanguinary sagas, *Twilight,* debuted at Thanksgiving 2008 and

took in $384 million worldwide. The follow-up, *New Moon,* was released on Nov. 20, 2009, and is expected to duplicate *Twilight's* success.

Television quickly cashed in: *True Blood,* starring Anna Paquin, above, gave HBO its first hit series since the glory days of *The Sopranos* and *Sex in the City.* As vampire fatigue set in, TIME reported in April 2009 that zombies were, uh, stirring back to life. Five months later, *Zombieland* was No. 1 at the box office.

Awards
And the Winner Is …

… Neil Patrick Harris, formerly TV's Doogie Howser, M.D., below. Harris, now a Broadway star, deployed his stylish wit as host of the 2009 Tony and Emmy telecasts, giving both shows a hefty ratings bump.

THE OSCAR AWARDS
Best Picture—*Slumdog Millionaire*
Best Director—Danny Boyle, *Slumdog Millionaire*
Best Actress—Kate Winslet, *The Reader*
Best Actor—Sean Penn, *Milk*

THE TONY AWARDS
Best Play—Yasmina Reza, *God of Carnage*
Best Musical—*Billy Elliott, The Musical*
Best Actor, Play—Geoffrey Rush, *Exit the King*
Best Actress, Play—Marcia Gay Harden, *God of Carnage*

THE GRAMMY AWARDS
Album of the Year—*Raising Sand,* Robert Plant and Alison Krauss
Song of the Year—*Viva La Vida,* Coldplay
Best Female Pop Vocal—*Chasing Pavements,* Adele
Best Male Pop Vocal—*Say,* John Mayer

THE EMMY AWARDS
Drama Series—*Mad Men,* AMC
Comedy Series—*30 Rock,* NBC
Actress, Drama—Glenn Close, *Damages,* FX
Actor, Drama—Bryan Cranston, *Breaking Bad,* AMC

Milestones

◻ A pop icon obsessed with shape-shifting, and a longtime TV newsman admired for his steadiness. An unlikely politician who brought People Power to the Philippines, and a writer who turned his acute powers of observation on everyday people. An affable second banana, an Irish American with heartbreaking stories to tell, and a repentant Secretary of Defense. All are among those whose lives we will recall long after 2009 has passed.

Trouper *Electrifying in concert, Michael Jackson dazzled British fans in 1992, despite a bandaged arm*

Proteus of pop *Jackson's startling physical evolution was the result of multiple plastic surgeries and skin bleaching (to address vitilgo, he said). Clockwise from top left: at age 9 in 1968; on tour in 1984; on trial in 2005; performing at the Super Bowl in 1993*

Michael Jackson

Fabulously gifted and perpetually preadolescent, the beloved, bewildering King of Pop leaves the stage

'M STARTING WITH THE MAN IN THE MIRROR," Michael Jackson sang in his 1988 hit. But over the years, the reflection he saw never stopped morphing. In recent years, the self-crowned King of Pop seemed so remote as to be extraterrestrial—the moonwalking moon child. But that was just the last of many Michaels who fascinated, seduced and troubled the world of popular music. In his first prodigious fame, at 11, as the Cupid and Kewpie doll of the Jackson 5, he was no more complicated than he was adorable: the family singing group's star, dimpled and lithe, a young emperor of elfin cool. Five of Katherine and Joe Jackson's nine kids were in the group, which had a slew of hits for Motown

Records, then went to Epic, called themselves the Jacksons and let Michael branch out on his own.

He recorded four solo albums and co-starred with Diana Ross in the movie of the Broadway hit *The Wiz*, before teaming with renowned producer Quincy Jones for 1979's *Off the Wall*. A mixture of disco, funk and plaintive ballads, the album defined MJ's style and sped him toward superstardom. The first single, *Don't Stop 'Til You Get Enough*, went to No. 1 and came with a fresh marketing tool: a music video, in which three Michaels appeared to perform intricate steps. It was the squall of an audiovisual genre that Jackson would shape and dominate.

All that was mere throat-clearing for 1982's classic *Thriller*, which would become the world's all-time best-selling album. Maturing as a songwriter, he turned a celebrity's denial of paternity into the whispery, groovy *Billie Jean* and a flee-don't-fight message into the unbeatable *Beat It*. The videos for these songs broke an informal color barrier at MTV, and the 14-minute superproduction for *Thriller* made videos the prime pop format of the 1980s.

Smash CDs followed, and his collaboration with Lionel Richie on the single and video *We Are the World* sold 7.5 million copies in the U.S. and raised more than $60 million for famine relief in Africa. He wowed 'em at the Super Bowl and with spectacular concert tours whose special effects never overwhelmed the slender dude with the gentle demeanor, dervish footwork and nonpareil showmanship. If you were a star in the '80s, you'd want to be Michael Jackson.

Yet it seemed as though *he* didn't want to be Michael Jackson. Plastic surgeons altered his face nearly beyond recognition. His cocoa skin was slowly blanched into a geisha's pancake white. He retreated to his palatial Neverland estate near Santa Barbara, Calif., and became the world's most reclusive exhibitionist.

Jackson had hoped to star in a Steven Spielberg film of *Peter Pan*, about the boy from Neverland who refuses to grow up. The story's reflection of his own needs, dreams and scars was poignant. In a tearful interview with Oprah Winfrey, he confessed that his father had beat him and called him ugly.

Once he had the money and power, the perpetually preadolescent Jackson moved into a fantasy version of childhood, in the company of young boys he saw as his peers and saviors. One of those boys brought a child-molestation civil suit against Jackson, which consumed the tabloids and ended only when he settled with the boy's family for a reported $20 million. In 2003, Jackson was charged with child molestation in criminal court. At his trial in 2005, he declared his innocence, once showing up in court in his pajamas. The jury agreed with him. He was never convicted of anything, except terminal weirdness, by a public that he now bewildered.

This Peter Pan died just as he was showing signs of adult behavior. Deeply in debt, he was forced to return to performing. He hadn't toured since 1997, yet he reluctantly agreed to a London gig that would eventually grow to 50 shows; more than $90 million worth of tickets were sold in advance. But on June 25, only hours after he wowed onlookers with an electrifying rehearsal for the London gig at L.A.'s Staples Center, he was rushed to a hospital, where he was pronounced dead at 50. As the news of his death traveled around the globe, fans gathered spontaneously to sing and dance his classic hits, millions of mirrors honoring a brilliantly gifted, deeply troubled and eternally fascinating man.

Left behind. The superstar's family carries on

Children
The star's three children attend the July 7 memorial service at the Staples Center in Los Angeles. From left: Paris, 11, and Prince Michael, 12. Prince Michael II, 7, known as "Blanket," is in front.

Brothers and Sisters
Jackson's siblings attend his Sept. 3 interment at Forest Lawn Memorial Park in Glendale, Calif. On Aug. 28, the Los Angeles County Coroner ruled Jackson's death a homicide, citing prescription drug abuse as the likely cause of his early demise.

Anchorman *Cronkite retired in 1981 and died at 92. At right, his reporting from Vietnam in 1968 fueled disillusionment with the war*

Walter Cronkite

Americans trusted the TV anchor, believing in his objectivity.
But in his most famous act, he delivered a personal opinion

NEWSMAN WALTER CRONKITE WAS SO THOR-oughly and uniquely linked with the word "trust" that it is tempting to say that the word should have been buried with him. In the generation since he left the anchor desk at the CBS *Evening News*, there were other public figures who inspired passion, devotion, confidence, intensity and personal identification. But trust, that milder but deeper sentiment—Cronkite owned it.

Middle America's favorite anchor was born in St. Joseph, Mo., and as he recalled in his memoir, *A Reporter's Life*, he developed a taste for reporting the news early. Living in Kansas City at age 6, he ran to a friend with a newspaper story about the death of President Warren Harding. "Look carefully at that picture," he told his friend. "It's the last picture you will ever see of Warren Harding." With typical self-deprecation, the elder Cronkite wrote, "I record it here today to establish my early predisposition to editorial work—to be both pontifical and wrong."

The Cronkite Americans came to know, though, was not a pontificator but an even-keeled newsman. After serving as a war correspondent in World War II and working for United Press in Europe after the war, he returned to the U.S. and joined CBS's TV news operation. When an ill-fated stint as a morning-show host collapsed, he became a fixture of CBS political coverage and began to anchor the evening news in 1962.

For two eventful, fitful decades—Kennedy, King and the another Kennedy were shot, Vietnam was fought and lost, Nixon resigned, hostages were taken in Iran—he was America's rock. He had a special bond with his audience, born of an on-air demeanor that was both folksy and knowing, calming but not uninterested.

Cronkite was TV's patron saint of objectivity, in an era when audiences still believed in it. And yet his most famous act as a news anchor was a rare occasion when he ventured an opinion. After reporting from Vietnam in 1968, Cronkite commented on the air that "it seems now more certain than ever that the bloody experience of Vietnam is to end in a stalemate." President Lyndon B. Johnson remarked that if he had lost Walter Cronkite, he had lost Middle America; soon after, L.B.J. declared he would not seek re-election.

Despite his comments on the war—or because of them—Cronkite cemented a reputation as a straight shooter. Maybe he benefited from working in a time when Americans simply had more trust in authority. But it may also be that he earned that trust—that by calling a quagmire what it was, he showed that a false evenhandedness that flies in the face of reality is not the same as honesty. What finally distinguished Walter Cronkite, perhaps, was not the trust his audience placed in him. It was that he was a good and wise enough newsman to place his trust in his audience. —*By James Poniewozick*

President Lyndon B. Johnson remarked that if he had lost Walter Cronkite, he had lost Middle America

Bookworm *Updike in the Boston Public Library. "In the world of my boyhood, there were books everywhere," he told* TIME

John Updike

Like Whitman, he told America's story—and America listened

THE CROWN OF "GREATNESS" NEVER SAT EASILY ON the snowcapped head of John Updike, one of the great writers of the 20th century, who died from lung cancer on Jan. 27 at the age of 76. He grew up a clever, stuttering child in small-town Pennsylvania and went to college at Harvard, where he served as head of the *Lampoon,* the campus humor magazine, rather than its storied literary magazine, the *Advocate.* His first published work in the *New Yorker* consisted of light verse.

But it was with the novel and the short story that he would have his lasting, lifelong romance. This appears to have dawned on Updike slowly, but it was abundantly clear by the publication of his second novel, *Rabbit, Run,* (1960) the first volume of five that chronicled the life of Rabbit Angstrom, Updike's great hero. Rather than a fictional alter ego, Angstrom was a vulgarian, a crass, lusty, middle-class salesman, through whom Updike anatomized and dramatized the great American spiritual and cultural crises of his generation.

Updike's hallmark was his glittering, gloriously vivid style. His talent for spotting detail, for capturing in prose the slightest shift in light or in a character's mood, was unmatched. He saw himself as more an artisan than an artist, and he produced nearly a book a year for much of his life—not just novels but short stories, book reviews, memoir and art criticism. His relentless curiosity sometimes led him to attempt experiments that were beyond his range. But at his best, as in the Rabbit novels or his 1968 foray into the sexual revolution, *Couples,* he looked deeply and clearly into the swamps of human experience and reported back to us what he saw with a matchless precision and a warm, generous judgment.

—*By Lev Grossman*

Corazon Aquino

For Filipinos, she will always be the saint in a yellow dress

CORAZON COJUANGCO WAS BORN INTO ONE OF THE wealthiest families in the Philippines. Fated to be married off in one dynastic match or another, she was instead courted by and fell in love with Benigno Aquino Jr., a brilliant and ambitious journalist whose popularity challenged the staus quo under dictator Ferdinand Marcos. In 1983 Aquino returned to the Philippines after three years of exile in the U.S., only to be shot dead even before he could set foot on the tarmac of Manila's international airport, and his devout and stoic Roman Catholic widow became the incarnation of a pious nation's dreams.

In December 1985 a Marcos-controlled court acquitted the military men accused of killing Benigno. Marcos then decided to hold a snap presidential election to reaffirm his mandate. Though hampered by the government's near monopoly of the media, Corazon Aquino's campaign attracted millions of fervent supporters, all decked out in yellow, the reluctant candidate's favorite color. When Marcos cheated her of victory in the February 1986 vote, the outcry was tremendous—and his doom was sealed. Millions crammed the streets to protect reformist soldiers who had mutinied against Marcos. Nuns armed only with rosaries knelt in front of tanks, stopping them in their tracks.

It was the first revolution to be fully televised. The world witnessed four days of military and civilian rebellion, a preview of similar uprisings that would later shake out the autocracies of Asia, Latin America, Eastern Europe and the Soviet Union. In a sweep of U.S. helicopters, Marcos was whisked off to exile in Hawaii, Aquino was proclaimed President of the Philippines—and TIME named her Woman of the Year at the end of 1986.

Benigno Aquino had warned before his murder that anyone unlucky enough to follow Marcos would be ousted within months. But his widow managed to last her entire six-year term. Furthermore, she retained a whiff of sanctity even as her government rotted. As Aquino ruled, every month seemed to diminish the political miracle of her astonishing rise to power, but still she survived. And her survival guaranteed the continuation of democracy in her homeland.

The Philippines is still a raucous political hothouse. But the dire days of deadly coup plots are over. At the end of her life, as she engaged in an excruciating battle with cancer, Corazon Aquino was the most revered figure in the Philippines. The country took out its yellow ribbons once again, bedecking trees and lampposts and even Facebook pages with the symbol of her revolution. And when she died, the Philippines and the world were reminded of the exemplary days of courage that she had embodied, the People Power uprising that would become a model for mass revolt at the end of the 20th century and into the 21st.

—*By Howard Chua-Eoan*

People's choice *Aquino in 1986, leading a revolution*

Frank McCourt

FOR MANY YEARS, FRANK MCCOURT TRIED AND FAILED TO WRITE about his early years. And no wonder: shortly ater he was born in Brooklyn, his impoverished parents returned to Ireland, where he survived a childhood fraught with horrors: his family, headed by an alcoholic father, was so poor that three of his six siblings died of disease and malnutrition. McCourt escaped to the U.S. and served in the Korean War, then used the G.I. Bill to get through college. It wasn't until he was in his 60s that the longtime New York City teacher found the key to telling his tale, writing in the detached voice of a child. The result, *Angela's Ashes,* was named for his mother. Published in 1996 when McCourt was 66, the best-selling memoir won a Pulitzer Prize.

Farrah Fawcett

THE 1970S BADLY NEEDED A SMILE. Watergate and Nixon's resignation, along with soaring crime rates and gas prices, had the nation in search of a tonic—which arrived in the trim form of a Texas blonde with a no-quit smile on the TV jiggle-fest *Charlie's Angels.* That would be Farrah Fawcett. In her last months, after a solid career of playing besieged TV-movie heroines, Fawcett served as another important emblem: the gaunt, glamorous fighter against anal cancer, struggling to spread awareness. A widely seen NBC TV special in May showed her final, brave battle with the disease.

Norman Borlaug

A SPECTER STALKED THE WORLD IN THE 1960s: the looming threat of mass starvation. As populations grew in the postwar years, farmers failed to keep pace—until the arrival of a humble plant scientist named Norman Borlaug.

In 1944, Borlaug joined the Rockefeller Foundation's effort to conquer hunger in Mexico. At the time, agricultural researchers were enhancing crop yields by bombing plants with nitrogen fertilizer. But they eventually discovered that the process made seed heads grow so big that they would collapse in the field. Nature seemed to have hit a wall.

In 1953, however, Borlaug found a wheat strain with a unique genetic trait: the stalk became stubby, but the seed heads would stay large. When Borlaug transferred the gene into tropical wheat, he created a plant that could yield huge heads of grain while maintaining stable growth rates. Using Borlaug's seeds, farmers could produce four times as much wheat per acre. The discovery ignited the Green Revolution, which helped eradicate famine in much of the world and earned Borlaug the 1970 Nobel Peace Prize. His work saved hundreds of millions of lives, and today half the world eats grains descended from his plants.

Andrew Wyeth

HE WAS THE GREAT PROBLEM of American modern art. He was a problem because he so completely refused to be modern in any terms that the art world cared about or could stomach. Long after it was no longer fashionable or even permissible to practice a flinty, granular realism, Andrew Wyeth went on making pictures with the kind of brushwork that specified the world in almost molecular detail. His virtuosity challenged the tenets of modernism. And he was popular at a time when popularity was out but, paradoxically, Pop Art was in.

He inherited his skills as a draftsman, and perhaps as a showman, from his demanding father, the popular illustrator N.C. Wyeth. Spare, quiet and somber, Andrew Wyeth's works seem to inhabit some prelapsarian America, the one that existed before automobiles and television, a lost nation of regions, localities and rural fastnesses. Which is why, even at their dryest and gravest, his pictures are inevitably flush with nostalgia. Yet their elusiveness and stillness command our eyes—and our respect.

Robert McNamara

AT THE BEGINNING OF HIS PROFESSIONAL CAREER, HE MADE A NAME FOR himself as the wunderkind who reformed the ailing Ford Motor Co. At the end, he tried to rehabilitate his reputation, as a do-gooder striving to save the globe's poorer nations as head of the World Bank. But Robert McNamara will always be best known for his role as the Secretary of Defense who was the architect of Washington's failed policy in Vietnam.

McNamara waited 30 years before conceding in his 1995 memoir, *In Retrospect: The Tragedy and Lessons of Vietnam,* that he had waged the war in error. But to those who came of age during the Vietnam War, McNamara's actions at the time will be recalled more than the words of contrition he uttered three decades later, after 58,000 Americans had lost their lives in Vietnam. The '60s protesters called that conflict "McNamara's war." Tens of thousands of them marched to protest against it, while young men burned their draft cards or fled to Canada to avoid the draft. McNamara admitted in his book that the U.S. government had never answered key questions that drove its war policy: "It seems beyond understanding, incredible, that we did not force ourselves to confront such issues head-on," he wrote.

Bea Arthur

"SASSY" IS THE WORD THAT COMES to mind when describing an actress like Bea Arthur and the characters she played, most notably on *Maude* and *The Golden Girls*. But sassy finally seems too small for Arthur, who died on April 25 of cancer at age 86. It connotes perkiness and feistiness; Arthur, on the other hand, exuded too much stature and presence to possess sassiness—even to need it, really. Physically (at five-nine), in her husky voice and in her imperious stature, she was a daunting presence, and even her nimblest one-liners seemed to vibrate up from deep in the earth. Sassy? She ate sassy for breakfast.

Merce Cunningham

THOUGH HE began his career as a soloist for the famed Martha Graham company in 1939, the great modernist choreographer struck out on his own in 1944, the beginning of his almost 50-year collaboration—both professional and personal—with composer John Cage. He strayed from Graham's romantic, balletic style and instead emphasized sudden changes of direction and insisted that the dance moves, musical score, set design and costumes all be prepared independently of one another. He died at 90 on July 26.

John Hope Franklin

WITH HIS GROUNDBREAKING 1947 book *From Slavery to Freedom,* John Hope Franklin bridged the gap between black history and American history, documenting how blacks and whites coexisted and how widely their experiences differed. Educated at the historically black Fisk University, Franklin earned two postgraduate degrees from Harvard and in 1995 received a Presidential Medal of Freedom and the NAACP's Spingarn Medal for his contribution to African-American history. He died at 94, on March 25.

Don Hewitt

WELL BEFORE HE CREATED *60 Minutes* in 1968, Don Hewitt was helping shape TV news, which in turn helped shape history. The show adapted the narrative form of great TV storytelling to the news, but while it brought the attention of millions to important stories and corruption reports (as well as entertainment stories), it also inspired a host of less-ambitious, ratings-driven prime-time news-magazines. Still, four decades later,

60 Minutes remains among one of TV's most-watched new shows: Hewitt's legacy keeps on ticking. He died on Aug. 19, age 86.

John Hughes

IN THE 1980S HE FLOURISHED AS the intimate chronicler, confidant and cheerleader of a generation of young people. Writing scripts that could have come from inside their muddled hearts, monitoring their rampaging hormones, John Hughes built a smart shelf of adolescent zeitgeist films: *Sixteen Candles, The Breakfast Club, Pretty in Pink* and *Ferris Bueller's Day Off.* Born in Michigan and raised in Illinois, Hughes never went Hollywood; his signature movies were written and filmed where he grew up. He generated successful movie-comedy franchises as fast as other people wrote postcards: first the *National Lampoon's Vacation* films,

then the teen movies, not a series but with more or less the same rep company of kids. And then the hit *Home Alone* series. He died at 59.

APPRECIATION

Karl Malden

MY FIRST MEETING WITH KARL, who died on July 1 at age 97, was in the office of the producer of *The Streets of San Francisco,* the '70s TV show. I'd been recommended for a part, and Karl was giving me the once-over. My dad [actor Kirk Douglas] told me what a hard worker Karl was. That was an understatement. Karl came from the steel mills of Gary, Ind. He taught me just how fortunate I was to be an actor. Early on in his career, Karl recognized that he was not going to be the leading man. But he was intent on being the best second lead there was. He had so many wonderful roles, in films from *A Streetcar Named Desire*—for which he won an Oscar—to *On the Waterfront.* I loved him and will miss him so.

—*Michael Douglas*

Ed McMahon

BEST KNOWN AS THE LONGTIME sidekick to Johnny Carson on *The*

Tonight Show, Ed McMahon died June 23 at 86. His Zen-like job was mainly to be Carson's companion. He was the brash voice of the show ("Heeeeeeeeere's Johnny!"), who bantered with Carson and gamely inhabited his yuk-it-up, good-guy persona. You gotta laugh: that was the message he sent to the public through the end. And though he made a career of his laugh—that big, booming, avuncular laugh—it is to McMahon's credit that he never made it seem like work.

Natasha Richardson

A DISTINGUISHED BRITISH ACTRESS who was a third-generation star of the noted Redgrave acting clan and the eldest daughter of the

great and controversial Vanessa Redgrave, Natasha Richardson died two days after a seemingly unremarkable fall while skiing in Quebec. She lost consciousness and within 24 hours was in three hospitals—the last in New York City, her adopted home, where Redgrave and other family members, including Richardson's actor husband Liam Neeson, stood loving watch. She was 45.

She could locate the befuddlement of a brainwashed heiress (in the movie *Patty Hearst*), the crassness of an old-time good-time girl (as Sally Bowles, a Tony-winning turn, in the 1998 Broadway revival of *Cabaret*), the desperation in a Tennessee Williams heroine (*Suddenly Last Summer* on TV; *A Streetcar Named Desire* on Broadway). She was a watchful actress, and always worth watching.

Patrick Swayze

HE HAD THE LOOKS, AND THE MOVES. As the star of some of the most iconic films of the 1980s and '90s— *Dirty Dancing, Ghost, Point Break* and that epic of B-movie machismo, *Road House*—Patrick Swayze brought intelligence and warmth to old-fashioned movie maleness. Then he played his most heroic role, in a gritty, dignified, very public 20-month battle with pancreatic cancer. The disease would have forced other men into retreat. But to prove to his fans (and maybe to himself) that cancer wouldn't stop him from living and working, Swayze took on the role of a craggy cop in the A&E series *The Beast.* His struggle ended on Sept. 14, when he died surrounded by wife Lisa Niemi and his family. He was 57.

A

AARP, 23
Abdul, Paula, 23
Abdullah, Abdullah, 66, 70
abortion, 101
abstract art, 112–13
ACORN, 53
adaptive reuse, 116
Adele, 123
Afghanistan, 64–67
  drug lords, 19
  elections, 66
  U.S. commitment in, 54, 64–67
  U.S. soldiers in, 6–7
African Americans
  Obama, Michele, and, 40
  racism against, 21
Afzali, Ahmad, 52
Agha-Soltan, Neda, 56, 61
Ahmadinejad, Mahmoud
  Iranian election and, 54, 56, 57, 59, 60, 62–63, 78
  nuclear power and, 81
  support for, 60
airplanes
  US Airways Hudson River crash, 4–5, 24, 44
Algren, Nelson, 108
American Idol, 23
Angela's Ashes (McCourt), 132
Anglican Church, 100
Anglo-Saxon artifacts, 92
anthropoids, 89
Apple, R.W., 64, 65
Apple Computer, 100
Aquino, Benigno, Jr., 131
Aquino, Corazon, 131
archaeology, 92
architecture
  adaptive reuse, 116
  Lincoln Center, 122
  narcotecture, 19
Arctic sea-ice pack, 92
Ardipithecus ramidus, 86–87
Arizona Cardinals, 106
Arlington National Cemetery, 50, 51
Armstrong, Lance, 82, 107
Arthur, Bea, 134
Art Nouveau, 113
Atlantis space shuttle, i
Australia
  drought, 92
  Australian Open, 102
Australopithecus afarensis, 86
automobile industry, U.S.
  bankruptcies, 31
  cash-for-clunkers plan, 30, 31
  Detroit and, 94–97
auto racing, 108
Axelrod, David, 29

B

Balchin, John, 92
Baling River Bridge, 72–74
baseball, 106
Basij, 56, 62–63
basketball, 103, 109
Batelle, John, 99
Baucus, Max, 33
Bay, Michael, 115
Beast, The, 135
Beat It, 127
Beatles, 110, 119

Beatles Rock Band game, 119
Beckett, Samuel, 118
Benedict XVI, Pope, 100
Berlin Wall, 14–15
Berlusconi, Silvio, 19, 80
Beyoncé (Knowles), 20
Bhutto, Benazir, 67
bicycle racing, 107
Biden, Joe, 29, 67
Billie Elliot, the Musical, 123
Billie Jean, 127
Bin Laden, Osama, 18, 65
Blavatsky, Madame, 113
Blomkamp, Neill, 114
Bloomberg, Michael, 116
Blue Mountain (Kandinsky), 112-13
Bo (White House dog), 36, 40
Bondy, Luc, 123
Bono, 110–11
Borel, Calvin, 104, 105
Bork, Robert, 48
Borlaug, Norman, 132
Bowie, David, 120
Boyle, Danny, 123
Boyle, Susan, 24–25, 120
Breaking Bad, 123
Britain, Libya and, 81
Britain's Got Talent, 24–25, 120
Broadway shows, 118, 123
Brown, Dan, 122
Bruni, Carla, 71
Bryant, Kobe, 103
bumpaholics, 19
Burress, Plaxico, 109
Bush, George H.W., 35
Bush, George W.
  Afghanistan and, 64
  Cowboys Stadium and, 108
  Iraq and, 69
  Kennedy, Ted, and, 48
Bush Administration
  automobile industry and, 31
  economic policy, 30
  foreign policy, 29
  interrogation methods, 18, 28
Butterfly Nebula, 91

C

Cage, John, 134
California
  economy, 43
  wildfires, 52
Calley, William, 19
Carson, Johnny, 135
Carter, Jimmy, 48
cash-for-clunkers plan, 30, 31
CBS *Evening News*, 129
Ceccacci, Tony, 91
Centers for Disease Control and
  Prevention (CDC), 84
CERN research center, 93
Chaotianmen Bridge, China, 75
Charlie's Angels, 132
Chasing Pavements (Adele), 123
Cheney, Dick, 67
Child, Julia, 101, 115
chimpanzees, 86
Chin, Denny, 98
China
  drought, 92
  economic stimulus package, 72–75
  environment, 75
  H1N1 virus, 84, 85

Christian Democratic Union
  party, Germany, 80
Chrysler, 31
CIA interrogation methods, 18, 19
Cink, Stewart, 103
Circuit City, 101
Clark, Raymond, III, 53
"Claw, the," 110–11
Clijsters, Kim, 20, 104
climate change, 92
Clinton, Bill
  health care reform and, 33
  North Korea and, 80
  Sotomayor, Sonia, and, 35
Clinton, Hillary
  in Middle East, 71
  in Moscow, 81
  Secretary of State, 29
  U.N. Security Council role, 19
Close, Glenn, 123
Colbert, Stephen, 121
Colbert Report, The, 121
Coldplay, 123
Colombia, 93
Comedy Central, 121
Conard, Nicholas, 88
Concerning the Spiritual in Art
  (Kandinsky), 113
Confederations Cup, 104
Contador, Alberto, 107
Cosmic Origins Spectrograph, 91
counterinsurgency, 67
counterterrorism, 67
Couples (Updike), 130
Cowboys Stadium, 108
Cowell, Simon, 23, 120
Craig, Daniel, 118
Craigslist murders, 53
Cranston, Bryan, 123
crime
  sports figures and, 109
  in U.S., 53
Cronkite, Walter, 128–29
Cunningham, Merce, 134

D

Dallas Cowboys, 108
Damages, 123
Dancing with the Stars, 22
Darwinius masillae, 89
David, Joshua, 116
Da Vinci Code, The (Brown), 122
DeGeneres, Ellen, 23
DeLay, Tom, 22
Democratic Party of Japan, 80
Democratic Party
  health care reform and, 33
  New York State, 43
Detroit, 94–97
Detroit Economic Growth Corpo-
  ration, 96
DiCaprio, Leonardo, 115
Diller Scofidio + Renfro, 116, 122
dinosaurs, 93
DioGuardi, Kara, 23
District 9, 114
Diversity (U.K. dance troupe), 120
Docter, Pete, 114
dog fighting, 109
Don't Stop 'Til You Get Enough, 127
Dorsey, Jack, 99
Douglas, Kirk, 135
Douglas, Michael, 135
drought, and climate change, 92

Dudamel, Gustavo, 119
Dugard, Jaycee Lee, 53

E

earthquakes
  in Italy, 12–13, 19
  in Sumatra, 80
economic issues
  in China, 74–75
  debate over in U.S., 26–27
  retail closings in U.S., 101
  stimulus plan in U.S., 30–31, 75
Emanuel, Ariel (Ari), 28
Emanuel, Ezekiel, 28
Emanuel, Rahm, 28, 38, 39, 70
Emmy Awards, 123
Ephron, Nora, 115
Episcopal Church, 100
Espada, Pedro, 43
Ethiopia, 86
evolution, 86–87, 89
Exit the King (Ionesco), 123

F

al-Faisal, Saud, 70
Fallon, Jimmy, 122
Favre, Brett, 109
Fawcett, Farrah, 132
Fecteau, T.J., 66
federal spending, U.S.
  economic stimulus plan and, 30
  health care reform and, 33
  protests against, 27, 30, 71
Federer, Roger, 82, 102, 104, 105
FedEx Cup, 109
Fiat, 31
Fisher Body assembly plant, 96–97
floods
  in Philippines, vi-1, 80
  in U.S. south, 52
Food, Inc., 115
food vendors, 19
football, 106, 108, 109
Ford, Henry, 31
Ford Motor Co., 31, 133
Foster, Amy, 101
France
  H1N1 virus and, 85
  Obama visit, 71
  Promenade Plantée, 116
Frank, Barney, 18
Franklin, John Hope, 134
French Open, 102
From Slavery to Freedom (Frank-
  lin), 134
funemployed, 19

G

G-8 summit, 71
G-20 summit, 81
Gaddafi, Muammar, 54, 81
Galbraith, Peter W., 66
Gandolfini, James, 118
Garrido, Nancy, 53
Garrido, Phillip Craig, 53
Gates, Henry Louis, Jr., 21
Gates, Robert, 28, 29, 77
gay marriage, in U.S., 101
Geithner, Timothy, 28
Gelb, Peter, 123
General Motors, 31
Gere, Richard, 23
Germanotta, Stefani Joanne (Lady

GaGa), 23
Germany
  Berlin Wall, 14–15
  elections of 2009, 80
  Messel Pit, 89
  Venus of Hohle Fels, 88
Gibbs, Nancy, 24-25
Gibbs, Robert, 29, 38, 39
Gilbert, Alan, 119
Giles, Hannah, 53
God of Carnage (Reza), 123
Going Rogue: An American Life
  (Palin), 42
Golden Gate Bridge, ii, iii
golf, 103
Goodman, John, 118
Gosselin, Jon, 22
Gosselin, Kate, 22
governors, U.S., 42–43
Graham, Lindsey, 34
Graham, Martha, 134
Grammy Awards, 123
Green Bay Packers, 109
Green Revolution, 132
Grossman, Lev, 122
Guggenheim, Solomon R.,
  Museum, 112
Guizhou Province, China, 72
Gutierrez, Nadya Denise Doud-
  Suleman ("Octomom"), 23

H

H1N1 virus, 82–85
  fatalities, 84
  in Mexico, 83, 84, 85
  number of cases, 85
  vaccine, 84, 85
Halderman, Robert, 22
Hamlet (Shakespeare), 118
Hammond, Robert, 116
Harden, Marcia Gay, 123
Harding, Warren, 129
Harris, Neil Patrick, 123
Hasan, Nidal Malik, 53
Hatch, Orrin, 48, 50
Hatoyama, Yukio, 80
health care reform, in U.S., 32–33
Henderson, Rick, 31
Herbert, Terry, 92
Hewitt, Don, 134
High Line Park, New York City,
  116–17
Hispanic Americans, 35
H.M.S. *Victory*, 92
Hocking, Scott, 97
Hohle Fels cave, Germany, 88
Holder, Eric, 28
Hollander, Justin, 96
Holmes, Santonio, 106
Honduras, 17
horse racing, 104, 105
House, Paul, 18
Hubble Space Telescope, 82,
  90–91, 93
Hudson River, plane ditch, 4–5, 44
Hughes, John, 134
human origins, 86–87, 89

I

Ida (primate fossil), 89
immigrants, illegal, 21
*In Retrospect: The Tragedy and
  Lessons of Vietnam* (McNamara),
  133

interrogation methods, 18, 19, 28
Iowa, gay marriage in, 101
iPhone, 100
Iran
  election protests, 8–9, 54, 56–61,
    62–63, 78
  nuclear power and, 81
  Twitter and, 99
  women in, 61
Iranian Americans, 61
Iraq
  Colbert Report in, 121
  Obama's address to Muslims
    and, 10–11
  U.S. withdrawal from, 68–69
Ireland, 132
Irwin, Bill, 118
Israel, 54, 55, 79
Italy
  earthquake, 12–13, 19
  elections, 80
  G-8 summit, 71

J

Jackman, Hugh, 118
Jackson, George, 96
Jackson, Joe, 126
Jackson, Katherine, 126
Jackson, Michael, 16–17, 125–27
Jackson, Paris, 127
Jackson, Peter, 115
Jackson, Phil, 103
Jackson, Prince Michael, 127
Jackson, Prince Michael II
  ("Blanket"), 127
Jackson, Randy, 23
Japan, 80
Jarrett, Valerie, 29, 37, 71
Jerusalem, 79
Jobs, Steve, 100
Joel, Billy, 23
Johns, Stephen, 53
Johnson, Codey, 66
Johnson, Jimmie, 108
Johnson, Katie, 38, 39
Johnson, Lyndon B., 32, 129
Johnson-Foster, Yolonda, 101
Jonas Brothers, 118
Jones, Jerry, 108
Jones, Jim, 29
Jones, Quincy, 127
Jon & Kate Plus Eight, 22
Jordan, Michael, 109
Julie & Julia, 101, 115
Jupiter, 93

K

Kandinsky, Wassily, 112–13
Karzai, Hamid, 66
Kazemi, Sahel, 109
Kennedy, Edward M. (Ted), 46–51
Kennedy, Edward M., Jr., 49, 50
Kennedy, Joan Bennett, 48, 49
Kennedy, Joe, 49
Kennedy, Joe, Jr., 49
Kennedy, John F., 48, 49, 129
Kennedy, John F., Jr., 50
Kennedy, John F., Presidential
  Library, 50, 51
Kennedy, Kara, 49
Kennedy, Patrick, 50
Kennedy, Robert F., 48, 49, 129
Kennedy, Victoria Reggie, 36, 48,
  49

Kenner, Robert, 115
Kentucky Derby, 104, 105
Kerry, John, 29
Khalid Sheikh Mohammed, 18
Khamenei, Ayatullah Ali, 56, 59,
  61
Khomeini, Ayatullah, 56
Kim Jong Il, 54, 80
King, Teresa, 18
Klein, Joe, 56, 65, 67, 78
Kopechne, Mary Jo, 48
Krauss, Alison, 123

L

La Brea Fire, California, 52
Lady GaGa, 23
Lagerfeld, Karl, 18
Lake Tai, China, 75
Lane, Nathan, 118
Langdon, Robert, 122
Lange, Jessica, 23
Large Hadron Collider, 93
Lario, Veronica, 80
Lasko, Regina, 22
*Late Late Show with Craig Fergu-
  son*, 122
Late Night with Jimmy Fallon, 122
Late Show with David Letterman, 22
Lauer, Matt, 19
Law, Jude, 118
Le, Annie, 53
Lee, Euna, 80
Leno, Jay, 122
Letterman, David, 22, 122
Lewis, Richard, 23
Libya, 54, 81
Lieberman, Avigdor, 79
Likud Party (Israel), 79
Lincoln Center, 122
Linens 'n' Things, 101
Ling, Laura, 80
Los Angeles Lakers, 103
Los Angeles Philharmonic, 119
Lost Symbol, The (Brown), 122
Lovejoy, C. Owen, 86
"Lucy" (*Australopithecus afarensis*),
  86
Luo Ping, 18
Luo Zhijun, 75
LuPone, Patti, 23

M

Maazel, Lorin, 119
MacLeod, Scott, 70
Mad Men, 123
Madoff, Bernard, 98
Madonna, 19, 23
Maersk Alabama, 45, 77
Maine, gay marriage in, 101
Malden, Karl, 135
al-Maliki, Nouri, 68–69
Marcos, Ferdinand, 131
Marine Corps, U.S., 77
Markoff, Philip, 53
Mayer, Catherine, 120
Mayer, John, 123
McCain, John, 42, 50, 67
McCartney, Paul, 119
McChrystal, Stanley, 65
McCourt, Frank, 132
McKiernan, David, 65
McMahon, Ed, 135
McNair, Steve, 109
McNamara, Robert, 66, 133

Medicaid, 31, 33
al-Megrahi, Abdel Basset Ali, 81
Messel Pit, Germany, 89
Metropolitan Museum of Art, 123
Meyer, Stephenie, 123
Micheletti, Robert, 81
Michigan Theatre, 94–95
Mickelson, Phil, 109
Middle Awash, Ethiopia, 86
Middle East
  conflicts, 54, 55, 79
  Obama's trip to, 70–71
Milk, 123
Milkmaid, The (Vermeer), 123
Mine That Bird (horse), 104, 105
Minnesota Vikings, 109
models, physique of, 18
Monserrate, Hiram, 43
Morgenthau, Robert, 35
Mousavi, Mir-Hossein, 56–59,
  62–63, 99
  profile, 78
movies, best/worst of, 114–15, 123
Moynihan, Daniel, 35
MTV Video Music Awards, 20
My Lai massacre, 19

N

Nadal, Rafael, 102
narcotecture, 19
NASA, 91
NASCAR, 108
National Sovereignty Day, Iraq, 68
NBA Hall of Fame, 109
Neeson, Liam, 135
Nelson, Horatio, 92
Netanyahu, Benjamin, 79
newspapers, closing of, 100
New York City
  art museums, 112–13
  food vendors, 116
  High Line Park, 116-17
  Lincoln Center, 122
  New York Philharmonic, 119
New York Giants, 109
New York Jets, 109
New York Yankees, 106
Nicholson, Marvin, 38, 39
Niemi, Lisa, 135
Nixon, Cynthia, 118
Nixon, Richard, 129, 132
North Korea, 54, 80
nuclear power, Iran and, 81

O

Obama, Barack, 80
  address to Muslims, 10–11, 70
  Administration, 28–29
  Afghanistan policy, 65–67
  automobile industry and, 31
  Colbert, Stephen, and, 121
  criticism of, 21, 27, 30, 71
  economic policy, 30–31
  foreign policy, 70–71
  Georgia floods and, 52
  H1N1 virus and, 84
  health care reform, 21, 32–33
  Inauguration, iv, v, vi, 2–3, 26
  Iran and, 61, 81
  Kennedy, Ted, and, 46, 49
  national mood and, 20, 33, 71
  Nobel Peace Prize, 70
  Olympic Games and, 108
  racism and, 21

Somali pirates and, 77
Supreme Court nomination, 35
talk to schoolchildren, 21
at the White House, 36–39
Obama, Malia, 37
Obama, Michele
in France, 71
profile, 40–41
at the White House, 37, 38
Obama, Sasha, 37
O'Brien, Conan, 122
Ocasek, Ric, 23
Octomom, 23
Odierno, Ray, 121
Odyssey Marine Exploration, 92
Off the Wall (Jackson), 127
O'Keeffe, Georgia, 112–13
O'Keefe, James, 53
Olympic Games, 108
Omega Centauri (NGC 5139), 91
Onyewu, Oguchi, 104
Open Championship, Britain, 103
O'Reilly, Bill, 121
Orlando Magic, 103
Oscar Awards, 123

P
Pakistan, 67
paleontology, 93
Palestinians, 54, 79
Palin, Sarah, 42
Pan Am Flight 103, 81
Paquin, Anna, 123
Paterson, David, 43, 44
Pearl River Delta, 74
Penn, Sean, 123
Perdue, Sonny, 52
Peterson, Bob, 114
Petraeus, David, 68
PGA Championship, 109
Philadelphia Eagles, 109
Philadelphia Phillies, 106
Philip, Prince, 18
Philippines
floods, vi-1, 80
leadership, 131
Phillips, Daniel, 45
Phillips, Lorrie, 45
Phillips, Mariah, 45
Phillips, Richard, 24, 25, 45, 77
pirates, Somalia and, 24, 45, 76–77
Pitino, Rick, 109
Pittsburgh Steelers, 106
Plant, Robert, 123
Polanski, Roman, 23
Potro, Juan Martin del, 102,
104-05,
Powell, Julie, 115
prehistoric humans, 88
primate fossils, 89
pro-life activists, 101
Promenade Plantée, 116
Putin, Vladimir, 71

Q
al-Qaeda, 52, 65, 67

R
Rabbit, Run (Updike), 130
racism, in U.S., 21
Rahnavard, Zahra, 78
Raising Sand (Plant, Krauss), 123
Raptorex kriegsteini, 93
rats, new species, 93

Reader, The, 115, 123
Reagan, Ronald, 48
reality television, 22, 23
Reaper drone aircraft, 77
Redgrave, Vanessa, 135
Rees, Roger, 118
Renta, Oscar de la, 40
Reporter's Life, A (Cronkite), 129
Republican Party
economic policy and, 30, 31
health care reform and, 33
New York State, 43
respiratory ailments, 84
retail store closings, in U.S., 101
Reza, Yasmina, 123
Richardson, Natasha, 135
Richie, Guy, 19
Richie, Lionel, 23, 127
Riedel, Bruce, 65, 67
Roberts, John, 3
Robinson, David, 109
Robinson, Marion, 40
Rockefeller Foundation, 132
Rock of Ages, 118
Rocky Mountain News, 100
Roddick, Andy, 102
Rodgriguez, Alex, 106
Roeder, Scott, 101
Roethlisberger, Ben, 106
Roman Catholic Church, 100
Roosevelt, Franklin D., 33
Ross, Diana, 127
Rumsfeld, Donald, 64–65
Rush, Geoffrey, 123
Russia
Obama visit, 71,
U.S. missiles and, 81

S
Samoa, 80
Sampras, Pete, 102
Sanford, Jenny, 43
Sanford, Mark, 18, 43
Sarkozy, Nicolas, 71
SARS virus, 84
State of Law party, Iraq, 69
Saudi Arabia, 70
Schlossberg, Caroline Kennedy, 49
Schuchat, Anne, 84
Schwab, James, 6–7
Schwarzenegger, Arnold, 43
Seattle *Post-Intelligencer*, 100
Sept. 11 terrorist attacks, 18
Series I, No. 4 (O'Keeffe), 113
Shi'ite Dawa Party, 69
Sirius Star, 76
60 Minutes, 134
Sloan, Jerry, 109
Slumdog Millionaire, 123
Smith, William Kennedy, 48
snakes, prehistoric, 93
Snowe, Olympia, 33
soccer, 104
social media, 99
Social Security, 33
Somali pirates, 24, 45, 76–77
Sotomayor, Sonia, 34–35
Souter, David, 35
South Pacific, weather and, 80
South Waziristan, 67
Spanish flu, 85
Spears, Britney, 110, 118
Spielberg, Steven, 127
Spitzer, Eliot, 43

Springsteen, Bruce, 23
Sprint Cup, 108
Starr, Ringo, 119
Station Fire, California, 52
Status of Forces Agreement, Iraq,
68
Stephan's Quintet (galaxies), 91
Stewart, Martha, 19
Stieglitz, Alfred, 113
Stockton, John, 109
Stone, Biz, 99
Streep, Meryl, 23, 115
Stringer, Vivian, 109
Sullenberger, Chesley B., II
5, 24, 44
sun, shuttle and, i
Super Bowl XLIII, 106
Supreme Court, U.S., 35
Swayze, Patrick, 135
Swift, Taylor, 20
swine flu. *See* H1N1 virus
Sypher, Karen, 109
Syria, 61

T
Taliban, 65, 67
Tanit, 77
"tea parties," 27, 30, 71
Tehran University, 62
Tehrik-i-Taliban, Pakistan, 67
Tennessee Titans, 109
tennis, 20, 102, 104
terrorism
in Pakistan, 67
plots, in U.S., 52
theater, best/worst of, 118, 123
Theosophy, 113
30 Rock, 123
This Is It (Jackson), 16–17
Thriller (Jackson), 127
Tiller, George, 101
Titanoboa cerrejonensis, 93
Tonga, 80
Tonight Show, The, 122, 135
Tony Awards, 123
Tosca (Puccini), 123
Tour Championship, 109
Tour de France, 107
*Transformers 2: Revenge of the
Fallen*, 114, 115
Tropical Storm Ketsana, 1, 80
Troubled Asset Relief Program
(TARP), 30
True Blood, 123
True Compass (Kennedy), 50
tsunamis, 80
Tumulty, Karen, 32
Turner, Kathleen, 118
tweets, 99
Twilight: New Moon, 123
Twilight series (Meyer), 123
Twitter
financing, 101
founders, profile, 99
Iran election and, 60

U
U2, 110–11, 118
underwater archaeology, 92
unemployment, in U.S., 19, 31
United Nations
climate change and, 92
nuclear inspections and, 81
Security Council, 19

United Service Organization
(USO), 121
Up, 114
Updike, John, 130
US Airways Flight 1549,
4–5, 24, 44
U.S. armed services
in Afghanistan, 6–7, 65
in Iraq, 71
Colbert, Stephen, and, 121
women in, 18
U.S. Holocaust Museum, 53
U.S. Navy SEALS, 77
U.S. Open (tennis), 20, 102, 104
U.S.S. *Bainbridge*, 77
U.S.S. *Halyburton*, 77

V
vampires, 123
vendrification, 19
Ventura, Jesse, 19
Venus of Hohle Fels, 88
Venus of Willendorf, 88
Vermeer, Jan, 123
Vick, Michael, 109
Vietnam War, 48, 66, 128, 129, 133
Viva La Vida (Coldplay), 123
Vogue, 18
von Brunn, James Wenneker, 53

W
Wagoner, Rick, 31
Waiting for Godot (Beckett), 118
waterboarding, 18, 19
Watson, Tom, 103
We Are the World, 127
Wedeman, Andrew, 75
Wesley, Anthony, 93
West, Kanye, 20
West Bank settlements, 55, 79
White, Tim, 86
Whitney Museum of American
Art, 112
Williams, Evan, 99
Williams, Hank, Jr., 23
Williams, Rowan, 100
Williams, Serena, 20, 104
Williams, Venus, 20, 104
Wilson, Joe, 21, 33
Wimbledon, 102, 104
Winfrey, Oprah, 127
Winslet, Kate, 115, 123
Wintour, Anna, 18
Woods, Tiger, 82, 104, 109
World Cup, 104
World Health Organization, 84
World Series, 106
Wyeth, Andrew, 133

Y
Yale University murder, 53
Yang, Yong-eun, 104
Yarborough, Cale, 108
Yosses, Bill, 38
Youngstown, Ohio, 96

Z
Zardari, Asif Ali, 67
Zazi, Mohammed Wali, 52
Zazi, Najibullah, 52
Zelaya, Manuel, 81
Zombieland, 123
zombies, 123